The PRINCIPLES OF DRIVING

The Principles of DRIVING

German National Equestrian Federation

KENILWORTH PRESS

First published in Great Britain 2002 by
Kenilworth Press Ltd
Addington
Buckingham
MK18 2JR

Translated from the 7th German language edition © 2002 FN Verlag der
Deutschen Reiterlichen Vereinigung GmbH, Warendorf, Germany

Completely revised edition (English language) © 2002 Kenilworth Press Ltd

© FN-Verlag der Deutschen Reiterlichen Vereinigung GmbH approves this
edition of 'Richtlinien für Reiten und Fahren, Band 5'

Previously published under the title 'Driving, The Complete Riding and
Driving System: Book 5'

First edition 1988

British Library Cataloguing in Publication Data
A catalogue record for this book is available from the British Library

ISBN 1-872119-45-X

Translation by Christina Belton

German text revised by Dieter Gross, Enno Georg, Bernhard Duen, Ewald
Meier, and Eduard von Below

Drawings by Barbara Wolfgramm and Uwe Spenlen

Endpaper photograph by Arnd Bronkhorst

Printed in Great Britain by MPG Books Ltd (www.mpg-books.co.uk)

Contents

ACKNOWLEDGEMENTS

The revision of this volume and the improvement of specialised sections was undertaken with the help of many experts in different fields.

Thanks are due to Dr Otger Wedekind, Wilfried Gehrmann and Ulrich Dommermuth for their suggestions.

Preface

German driving is renowned the world over, not only because of the numerous successes achieved by German drivers in all branches of the sport, but also, and most importantly, because of the logical, progressive training system which it provides for both drivers and horses. As a result of extensive trials, especially by the English driving teacher Edwin Howlett, the driving system devised by Benno von Achenbach received official recognition in 1922. Since then it has been the standard system in use in Germany.

In the modern industrial world the horse has become obsolete as a working animal, yet in the sport and leisure sectors it has enjoyed a revival on a scale which has exceeded all expectations. The sport of driving is represented by numerous national and international organisations.

Leisure and potential competition drivers do not necessarily come from a 'horsy' background, so thorough, systematic training is especially important. This should cover harness, harnessing, putting-to and the use of the aids. Drivers must be trained in such a way that they do not, through ignorance of correct harnessing or driving technique, cause suffering or injury to the horse or endanger other drivers or road users.

The basic principles of the Achenbach system:

The official instruction handbooks of the German Equestrian Federation are based on classical teachings. They are the basis for the training of all riders, drivers, vaulters, trainers and judges committed to adhering to classical principles.

GERMAN FN SPORT DIVISION

THE HORSEMAN'S DUTIES TO HIS HORSE

1. Anyone who takes charge of a horse assumes responsibility for the living creature entrusted to his care.

2. The horse's management should reflect its inherent needs.

3. Whatever the horse is used for, the utmost importance should be attached to its physical and mental well-being.

4. Every horse should be treated with the same consideration, irrespective of its race, age and gender, or whether it is used for breeding, leisure or competition.

5. Our understanding of the horse's history and lifestyle, and our knowledge of handling and dealing with horses are part of our cultural heritage. They should be safeguarded and passed on, and handed down to future generations.

6. Contact with horses makes a lasting impression and has a character-forming effect especially on young people. These positive effects should be encouraged and built on.

7. The rider, who is the horse's partner, must submit both himself and the horse in his charge to a programme of training. The aim of this training is the greatest possible harmony between man and horse.

8. The use of the horse for competition or leisure riding, driving or vaulting must be in keeping with its type, its ability, its training and its level of fitness. Trying to improve the horse's performance through the use of drugs or unhorsemanlike practices is unacceptable.

9. The horseman's responsibility for the animal entrusted to him continues until the end of its life. The decisions made must always be based on what is best for the horse.

1

General Considerations

Equine nature

An understanding of equine nature is a basic requisite for every driver. Only if you strive constantly to understand the nature of horses will you be able to act appropriately when you are around them.

The horse is a **herd animal**. The herd unit offers it protection and security. No horse likes to be alone – this is something it needs to be introduced to carefully. In training, we can make use of the herd instinct, for example by putting an older, more experienced horse in the lead.

Horses have a **strict 'pecking order'** or herd hierarchy. Rules within the herd society ensure the survival of the herd. Fights to establish the pecking order are part of the horse's instinctive behaviour. They are commonest among youngsters, but are also seen when a new horse is put out in the field. Horses use their feet and teeth to defend themselves. They can be quite ruthless. On the other hand, they show sensitivity in their relationships with each other, and curiosity and affection also feature prominently in their behaviour.

Everyone who has to do with horses must be aware that even in horse/human relationships, horses need to establish a pecking order. Only if you behave in a calm, firm and logically consistent manner will you be accepted by the horse as a higher-ranking being.

Horses are **creatures of flight**. For herbivores, immediate flight offers the best protection against all forms of danger. However, different horses have different stimulus thresholds, and uncertainty or loss of confidence can trigger this flight behaviour. A panicking horse may be oblivious to all outside influences, and as such it can be dangerous.

A tendency to shy is an unpleasant consequence of the horse's avoidance-and-flight behaviour. It is pointless to punish the horse for this instinctive reaction. Calm, patient familiarisation with as many new situations as possible will build the horse's confidence and sense of security. In the wild, horses were always **on the move**. In their original habitat, the huge expanses of the steppes, they moved about for many hours of the day finding food. Hence exercise, light, fresh air and contact with other horses are important for the horse's well-being. Special attention should be paid to these criteria when keeping horses in stables, and in their daily care and handling. Horses should be allowed sufficient and varied exercise, and this should include being turned out in a field or exercise area.

Every horse is different in its **character** and **temperament**, likes and dislikes. The horse's moods and intentions can be interpreted through its body language, for example by its ear or tail movements or the expression in its eyes.

Horses are not naturally aggressive to those around them, although they are often rough with each other, especially stallions. Handling problems are usually due to incorrect handling and bad experiences.

The driver must be patient, observant and prepared to spend time learning to interpret the horse's behaviour correctly. Only then will the horse come to have confidence in him and like him. In time the driver will be able to distinguish between fear and resistance, and to act correctly in his training and education of the horse.

The carriage horse's training is judged not only by the quality of its paces when being driven, but also by whether it has retained its spontaneity and individuality.

Horses which are contented and ready to give of their best in their day-to-day work best meet the criteria for a **stable, harmonious relationship between man and horse**. These foundations will be strengthened and developed through patience, psychological understanding and frequent praise.

THE DRIVER

Handling and driving horses require certain **qualities in the driver**. These qualities become further established and developed as training progresses. A **love of animals** and an ability to **empathise** are required, as well as **patience, self-control, fairness** and **discipline**. The driver is responsible for his equine partner. He must be constantly prepared to learn, and ready to look for faults first in himself, and not in the horse.

Theoretical knowledge enhances the enjoyment of driving. A knowledge of equine nature and behaviour, and of handling and dealing with horses, as well as of the theory of driving and the principles of training, are obvious necessities for the serious, responsible driver.

THE SCHOOL HORSE

A suitable school horse or 'schoolmaster' is one of the most important prerequisites for teaching driving.

The school horse should have an equable, calm **temperament** (it should be 'quiet'). It should work with 'looseness' (*Losgelassenheit*) and should come onto the aids easily. A horse which has been schooled and suppled equally on each rein, and is confident and established in its way of going provides the best foundation for learning to drive.

School horses often work long hours. For this reason, and also because they are driven by so many different people, they should be treated with care and respect, and they require **careful management and handling**. This should include being driven occasionally by an instructor or other experienced driver in order to check, and if necessary re-establish their looseness and suppleness (German: *Durchlässigkeit*, or ability to 'let the aids through').

The reputation and standing of a training establishment are based on the quality of its school horses.

THE INSTRUCTOR

Instructors, and trainers, have an especially responsible and varied role in the sport of carriage driving. Students and horses, with their different aptitudes, have to be trained and improved in accordance with the principles of the Achenbach system, and the students must also be taught to handle horses safely and correctly.

This task requires **a particularly high degree of practical driving skill and experience**, which should be derived from riding and/or driving as many different horses as possible and taking part in different equestrian pursuits and disciplines.

The instructor should be willing and able to imagine himself in the student's place so that he can use his expert knowledge and empathising skills to correct faults and enable the rider to progress.

Practical experience and **an aptitude for teaching** are essential. Also, every trainer and instructor must be aware of the position he holds: he must **set an example** not only in his driving and handling of horses but also in the way he behaves.

Until the basic principles have been learned and have become established, the student needs to have one instructor he can relate to. If the instructor is changed suddenly or too soon, confusion can result.

Advanced level drivers, and even top level competitors, also need to be corrected constantly by experienced professionals in order to combat the faults which can develop only too easily when working unsupervised.

A **qualification in instructing**, obtained by passing the appropriate examination, should be a 'must' for anyone working as an instructor. In Germany there are qualifications for **amateur** as well as professional instructors. These are obtained by taking the graded tests in the various areas of activity, and they lead to different levels of responsibility.

In Germany the requirements for passing these tests are laid down in the *Ausbildungs- und Prüfungs-Ordnung* published by the Deutsche Reiterlichen Vereinigung e.V. (FN), Warendorf, Germany.

THE TRAINING AREA

The **theoretical instruction** goes hand in hand with the practical training. Some of this will take place in the stable (for example, clipping and trimming, bandaging, harnessing and discussions on conformation, etc.) or the school, but a suitable 'classroom' should also be available. Training videos and a video camera (camcorder) are a useful adjunct and will make the training more interesting and effective.

The practical training should be carried out in a suitable, enclosed outdoor school or arena. This is safer for the beginner since he is not yet fully in control, and it cuts out most of the distractions which could upset the horse.

The school and the stable yard are the 'showpiece' of any riding establishment. As well as **cleanliness** and **tidiness** in all areas, the riding surface and the obstacles (cross-country and obstacle-driving) need regular care and attention.

THE DRESSAGE ARENA AND THE SCHOOL

DRESSAGE ARENA

Arena markers

To help prevent misunderstandings a standardised system of arena markers and rules is used.

An arena used for driven dressage tests can be either 40m x 80m or 40m x 100m in size.

The markers are as follows:

- The letters A and C mark the middle of the two short sides.

- The letters B and E (also known as the 'half markers') are found in the middle of the long sides.

- The markers M, F, K and H are on the long sides 10m from the ends of the school. D and G are level with these, on the centre line.

- The letters P, V, R and S are on the long sides of the 40m x 100m arena, 30m from the ends. The letters 'I' and 'L' are level with these, on the centre line.

- In addition to these, the 'circle points' (shown on the diagram with a black dot) are the points where the 40m circle touches the side of the arena. The circle points on the long sides of the 40m x 80m arena are also known as the 'quarter markers'.

- The centre point of the arena is known as 'X'.

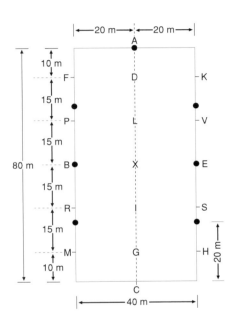

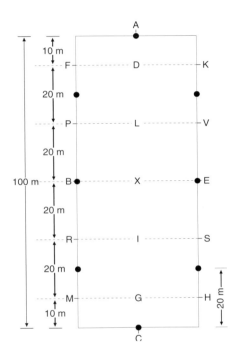

Arenas for driven dressage

THE SCHOOL

This should be at least 70m x 120m. Cones and poles should be available for simulating roads or building obstacle courses of different standards and degrees of difficulty.

CODE OF PRACTICE FOR CROSS-COUNTRY DRIVING

Driving across country plays an important part in the driver's basic training. As well as possessing the requisite driving skills, the driver needs to be familiar with the basic code of conduct for driving in the country.

As a **visitor** to the countryside he must always behave in such a way that he makes only friends, not enemies. Not all drivers have the advantage of direct access to the countryside from their stables. It is in the rider's own interest to keep the dangers and risks of driving outside to the minimum.

On **safety grounds**, the condition, fit and suitability of the harness and vehicle must be checked before each outing.

Driving on footpaths and cycle tracks can damage them, and should therefore be avoided, as should driving on tracks made soft by rain or frost.

The **pace** should be suited to the situation and the conditions. Walkers, cyclists, riders and motor vehicles should be passed if necessary in walk.

When driving on field or woodland tracks, the gait and pace should depend on the following:

- the surface

- weather conditions

- whether you can see clearly what lies ahead

- the driver's level of training

- the horse's level of training.

If any damage is done during the drive, it must be reported immediately to the landowner so that compensation can be agreed.

When driving on public roads and tracks, the groom or passenger should, when instructed by the driver, use a signalling disc to communicate intentions to other road users.

HARNESS, DRESS AND EQUIPMENT

DRESS AND EQUIPMENT FOR THE DRIVER

Unlike riding, no specialised clothing is required for learning to drive. The only requirement is that it should be suitable for a horsy environment, that is it should be hard-wearing and easy to care for, and should allow the necessary freedom of movement. Baggy, flapping clothes can get caught up on things. Shoes should be sturdy and cover the whole foot: sandals and very lightweight shoes offer no protection against injuries caused by the horse's feet or the wheels of the carriage. A pair of leather gloves is recommended. These should be sufficiently roomy, and the fingers should be of the correct length.

In driving competitions and performance tests, the rider and groom or passenger should be dressed appropriately for the turnout and the competition or test. In

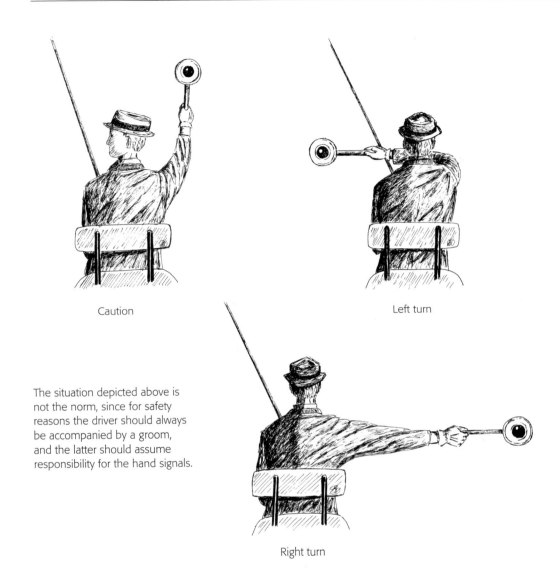

Caution

Left turn

The situation depicted above is not the norm, since for safety reasons the driver should always be accompanied by a groom, and the latter should assume responsibility for the hand signals.

Right turn

Germany, details can be found in the '*LPO*', or *Leistungs-Prüfungs-Ordnung*' (the rules for competitions and performance tests). In all cases the driver should carry a whip which is of the correct design and can be used effectively – that is, it should be comfortable to hold and the stick should be long enough for the driver to be able to apply the whip next to the pad.

The 'apron' or 'rug' serves to protect the driver's clothing from the greased reins. It also prevents the reins falling between the driver's legs. It should reach half way down the lower leg, and may consist of a small woollen blanket or it may be made of thick drill, linen or a synthetic material, and be tailored to fit. In sporting driving and competitions, the colour should tone in with that of the vehicle and seat cushions.

HARNESS AND EQUIPMENT FOR THE HORSE

Types of harness

There are two types of harness: breastcollar harness and full collar harness (collar harness). Breastcollar harness can be adjusted to fit a lot of different horses. The collar of a full collar harness, on the other hand, must be shaped exactly to fit the individual horse's neck, shoulders and breast. It is of limited used on other horses.

A bridle with 'Achenbach-style' reins is used with both breastcollar and full collar harness.

Driving bridle and bits

The driving bridle is made up of the following parts:

1. the headpiece, with the blinker stay buckle attached,

2. face drop (face piece),

3. browband (with chain decoration and rosettes),

4. cheekpieces with blinkers and blinker stays attached (the latter reinforced with wire to hold the blinkers in position, i.e. pointing outwards slightly),

5. throatlatch or throatlash, with buckle at each end,

6. noseband, with 1–3 loops (keepers) or vertical slots (to allow the position of the cheekpieces to be varied).

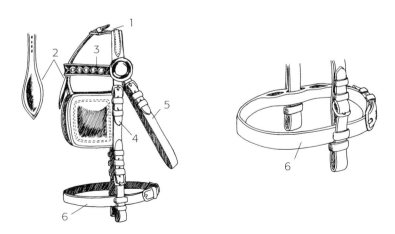

The browband must be long enough to allow the headpiece to sit comfortably behind the horse's ears without rubbing them. The blinkers – also known as winkers or blinders – prevent the horse from seeing the whip coming. Without them, an excitable horse will be upset by every movement of the driver's hand, and a lazy horse, on the other hand, will watch the driver and only go forward when it sees the whip hand raised. With pairs and teams it is not possible to drive correctly, in a manner designed to minimise strain on the horses, and with the work correctly distributed, unless the horses are wearing blinkers. Rarely are two or more horses so alike in temperament and other characteristics that these problems do not arise. Fitting and putting on a driving bridle requires special care because of the blinkers.

Blinkers are made of firm leather and are square with rounded corners, with a slight outward bulge on a level with the horse's eyes. They owe their rigidity to a metal or plastic plate sewn into them. Correctly fitted blinkers point outwards slightly and are held in position by the blinker stays, which are straps made of sturdy leather, if possible reinforced with wire. These are sewn onto the blinkers at one end and fastened at the other to a buckle attached to the headpiece.

The blinkers must be attached to the cheekpiece throughout their length. The outward bulge on the blinkers, referred to above, must be in the upper third of the blinker so as to leave enough room for the eye. Blinkers which are too close restrict the horse's vision and can cause the eyelashes to press against the eye, resulting in considerable pain. Blinkers which are too small or made of soft or floppy leather are useless.

The cheekpieces should be in line with the bit, which is achieved by passing them through the appropriate slots in the noseband. The 'face drops' which hang below the browband are used to make all the horses look alike from the front in spite of different face markings. The off- and near-horse's bridles can be told apart by the buckle and the slots on the noseband: the three slots (the adjustable side) should be on the inside.

The bits most commonly used for driving are:

1. the double ring ('Wilson') snaffle (with jointed mouthpiece),

2. the curb with unjointed mouthpiece (various designs),

3. the curb with jointed mouthpiece, which is a cross between the above types (see list of permitted bits).

Whichever bit is used, the first priority is that it should fit the shape of the horse's mouth. The Wilson snaffle has one fixed and one loose or 'floating' ring at each end, i.e. 'double rings'. By attaching the rein to both or just one ring, the action of the bit can be varied from mild to severe.

Some curb bits have a sliding cheek, that is the mouthpiece can be slid a little way up and down the cheekpiece.

Note: When attaching the rein to both rings of the double-ring snaffle (mild action), the cheekpieces should not be passed through the slots in the noseband. Anchoring the noseband to the cheekpieces in this way would serve to transfer most of the action of the bit onto the horse's nose.

This has the advantage that the bit changes its position whenever the horse moves its mouth, helping to prevent the horse becoming 'dead' in its mouth. However, it can also cause injury to the lips.

The lever action of the curb bit is based on the resistance produced by the curb chain. The severity of the action can be adjusted by attaching the rein in different positions on the cheekpiece of the bit: the lower the point of attachment, the more severe the action. The mildest lever action is obtained by fastening the reins around the cheek just below the mouthpiece.

PERMITTED DRIVING BITS AND AUXILIARY AIDS FOR GERMAN COMPETITION DRIVING

(Illustrations taken from Para B.1/11 of the German competition rules)

1. All types of competition (Categories C and B)

The following applies to all the bits illustrated:
Port, arch, half-moon or tongue-groove: 0-30mm.
The cheekpieces of bits may be shortened.
A bottom cross-bar is permitted.

Minimum thickness all bits, measured at the corners of the mouth:
Horses: 14mm   Ponies: 10mm.

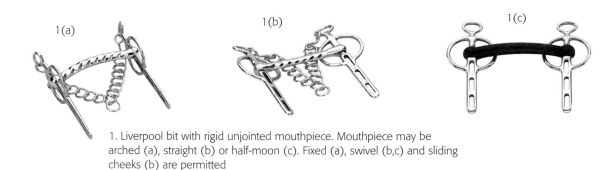

1(a)   1(b)   1(c)

1. Liverpool bit with rigid unjointed mouthpiece. Mouthpiece may be arched (a), straight (b) or half-moon (c). Fixed (a), swivel (b,c) and sliding cheeks (b) are permitted

2

2. Liverpool bit with 'KK Conrad' port (NB: Must be fitted so that ends of the mouthpiece are just touching the corners of the mouth)

3. Single-jointed Liverpool bit. The double-jointed form is also permitted, as is the concave form (shaped to the tongue), similar to illustration 2 in the (German) list of permitted riding bits

3

4. Liverpool bit with bottom cross-bar

5. Two-ring and three-ring butterfly pelham ('knuckleduster'). Also permitted with mouthpieces described in captions to illustrations 1, 2 and 3

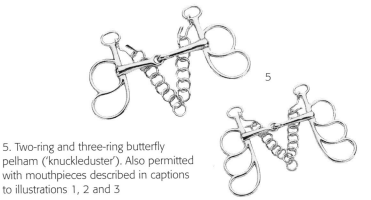

6. Elbow bit (army reversible/angle-cheek pelham). Also permitted with mouth-pieces described in captions to illustrations 1, 2, 3 and 4

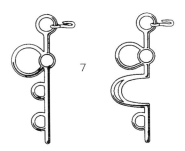

7. Gig bit or Tilbury, and Buxton bit. Also permitted with mouthpieces described in captions to illustrations 1, 2, 3 and 4

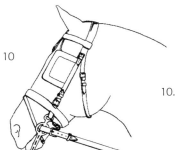

8. Double ring or Wilson snaffle (also permitted with indented outer ring – 'Esterhazy Jucker snaf-fle' – or with unjointed rubber mouthpiece) or sin-gle-ring snaffle (see permitted bits for German ridden dressage, illustrations 1-5)

9. Curb chain; a curb guard is permitted

10. Driving bridle with blinkers

2. *Cross-country, marathon and obstacle competitions, Categories B and A (additional to 1)*

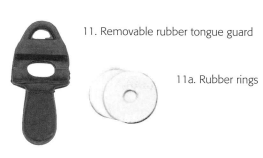

11. Removable rubber tongue guard

11a. Rubber rings

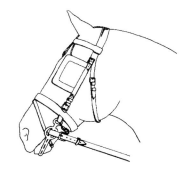

12. Driving bridle with 'flash' noseband (in Cat.B may only be used with a double ring snaffle): permitted for cross-country only

3. *All types of Category A competitions: Optional; bitless bridles not permitted*

Any bit, but especially a curb, must be fitted with the utmost care. Since the shape of the jaw and the size of the mouth is different in every horse, bits must always be fitted individually. The most important thing to look for in a bit is that the mouthpiece is the correct width for the horse's mouth and that it lies correctly on the lower jaw. The upper cheek of the bit should be bent outwards so that the bottom of the cheekpiece of the bridle does not chafe the horse. The curb hooks should be bent outwards, with the opening at the front. The proper fitting and action of the bit depends on the curb hooks being bent correctly. Curb hooks which are misshapen or fitted the wrong way round (for example, the right hook on the left side of the bit) cause injury to the horse's mouth.

Stainless-steel bits are recommended. Brass breaks too easily. With alloys it is difficult to know which are reliable. Rubber bits should always have a steel core.

Breastcollar harness for singles and pairs

BREASTCOLLAR HARNESS FOR SINGLE TURNOUT

Compared with pairs harness, the breast piece of the breastcollar used with single harness is shorter, and the pad is constructed differently. The position of the breastcollar is adjusted by means of a buckle, or buckles, on the neckstrap. Narrow breastcollars are incorrect because they cut into the chest and cause the horse pain (the recommended width is 9cm). The top part of the neckstrap is wider and may be padded. It lies on the neck just in front of the withers and slopes backwards slightly from bottom to top. There is a buckle at each end of the breast piece for the attachment of the traces. With some harness the traces are sewn onto the breastcollar. In this case the buckle for adjusting the length should not be on the last third of the trace because it could catch on the tail hairs and pull them out, or could touch the hind leg and cause soreness or injury, or make the horse kick. These problems do not arise if the trace is buckled directly onto the breast piece, in front of the pad. Provided the harness is adjusted correctly, the shaft cannot press the trace buckle against the horse's side and cause soreness because the buckle should lie below the level of the shaft.

In single harness the saddle, or pad, has to take the weight of the shafts, so it is wider and more strongly constructed than the pad used with pairs harness. As with a riding saddle, the top part of the saddle or pad used in single harness is built on a rigid tree made of metal, leather or a synthetic material. The sides are padded so as to provide the necessary clearance over the withers. The bottom part of the pad consists of a girth, which should not be too narrow.

For maximum safety the backband should be made out of a single piece of leather. With a single-axle vehicle, the backband is not attached to the saddle or pad, but is free to slide through it from side to side. This enables it to absorb the sideways movements of the shafts.

Two different kinds of tugs can be used, depending on the type of vehicle. With four-wheeled vehicles, only the weight of the shafts is borne by the tugs. With two-wheeled vehicles there is more strain on the backband and tugs. The tugs used with a four-wheeled vehicle – Tilbury tugs – are made of metal, while those in use on two-wheeled vehicles are constructed of several layers of strong leather sewn together. With both two- and four-wheeled vehicles, the tugs are connected by the belly band, which is held in position by a loop sewn onto the girth.

Terrets, or rein guides, take the form of fixed rings screwed into the sides of the pad near the top, and loose rings attached to the neckstrap. These enable the driver to maintain a steady contact with the horse's mouth. Between the two pad terrets is a hook for the attachment of bearing reins.

The crupper, consisting of a backstrap with two buckles, and a dock piece, is attached to a 'D' on the back of the pad. The protruding points of the straps on the backband should be secured, and the buckle parts designed to prevent the reins catching on or under them. The dock piece should be sewn onto the backband: if buckles are used the tail hairs can catch on them. The dock is padded where it passes under the horse's tail so that the tail is raised slightly. This helps prevent the horse clamping its tail on the reins and trapping them.

In hilly areas or for increased safety a breeching can be used with single harness. The top edge of the breeching body should be a hand's width below the point of the buttock. If it is too low it will restrict the horse when it halts or reins back. It should be adjusted in such a way that when the horse is stood up in his traces a fist can be

Breastcollar Harness for Single Turnout

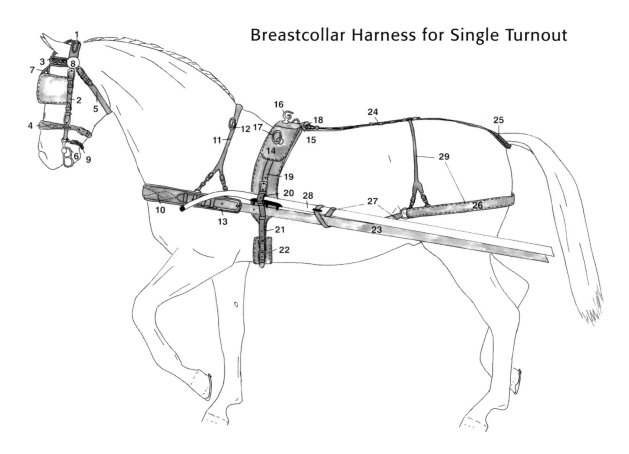

1. Headpiece with winker stay buckle
2. Cheekpiece with blinkers and winker stays
3. Browband with decorative chain
4. Noseband with slots and loops
5. Throatlatch or throatlash
6. Bit (butterfly pelham)
7. Face drop
8. Rosette
9. Curb chain
10. Breaststrap of breastcollar
11. Neckstrap of breastcollar
12. Terret
13. Trace buckle
14. Skirt
15. Saddle or pad
16. Bearing hook
17. Pad terret
18. Crupper 'D'
19. Backband
20. Tug (open tug with two-wheeled vehicles, Tilbury tug with four-wheeled vehicles)
21. Girth
22. Belly band
23. Trace
24. Crupper backstrap
25. Crupper dockpiece – sewn to back-strap
26. Breeching body
27. Breeching strap
28. Shaft
29. Breeching

Breastcollar Pair Harness

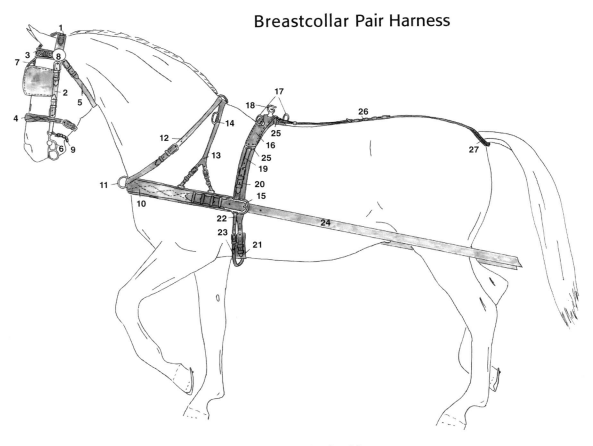

1. Headpiece with winker stay buckle
2. Cheekpiece with blinker and winker stay
3. Browband with decorative chain
4. Noseband with slots and loops
5. Throatlatch or throatlash
6. Bit (butterfly pelham)
7. Face drop
8. Rosette
9. Curb chain
10. Breaststrap of breastcollar
11. Pole strap ring
12. Yoke strap
13. Neckstrap
14. Terret
15. Tug buckle
16. Pad
17. Pad terret
18. Bearing hook
19. Pad strap point
20. Pad strap
21. Girth
22. False belly band point
23. False belly band
24. Trace
25. 'D' for pad strap point
26. Crupper backstrap
27. Crupper dock piece – sewn to backstrap

inserted between the breeching and the horse's body below the point of the buttock on either side.

With single harness, if no breeching is fitted a kicking strap should be used. The kicking strap passes through a loop on the rear third of the crupper backstrap and attaches at the sides to 'D's provided for this purpose on the shafts. The kicking strap is designed to prevent the horse kicking out.

BREASTCOLLAR HARNESS FOR PAIRS

Pair harness differs from single harness in that there is a loose steel ring for the pole strap sewn onto the breastcollar, and the pad is constructed differently. The pole strap ring is offset to the inside of the collar, on the side of the pole, and the near and off horses' collars can be told apart by the position of the rings.

Additional support for the breastcollar can be provided by fitting a yoke strap, which passes through a loop on the neckstrap and through the pole strap rings. The buckle on the yoke strap should be on the outside. A yoke strap is helpful for reining back and when driving multiples because of the extra weight of the main and lead bars, or the swing pole.

The girth is buckled onto the pad and holds it in position. Also attached to the pad, instead of a free-running backband, is the pad strap. This should be adjusted so that the trace runs in a straight line to the swingle tree or splinter bar. The tug buckle has a 'D' on the bottom for the attachment of the false belly band, which should be adjusted so that the alignment of the trace is not disturbed by the horse's trotting movement. If you can insert a fist between the false belly band and the horse's body the adjustment is about right. The false belly band should do up on the left side on the nearside horse and the right side on the offside horse so that both buckles are within reach when the horses are attached to the vehicle. If there are buckles on both ends of the girth, the one on the outside should be used.

When driving cross-country or in hilly areas it is advisable to use a breeching, though on pairs harness this is attached to the tug buckles. Trace carriers are not necessary if the traces and pole strap are adjusted correctly in relation to each other. The other parts of the harness are of the same design and used in the same way as single harness.

Pole straps are an essential part of pairs' harness. They are constructed of two layers of best quality leather sewn together, and run from the pole head to the pole strap rings on the breastcollars. They fasten with a buckle. Pole straps serve to steer the pole, and also for braking. Pole chains (as opposed to straps) should not be used with breastcollar harness, they do not fit in with the style, and so spoil the general impression.

Trained horses should be as close as possible to the pole whilst remaining straight. The inside trace runs parallel to the shaft from the tug buckle to the swingle tree. The outside trace 'takes a longer course' (about 5cm longer) from the tug buckle to the swingle tree because of the range of movement of the horse's quarters. On single harness the average length of the traces is 2.30m, and on pair harness 1.95m. The exact length depends on the size of the horse and the height of the swingle tree or splinter bar.

Collar harness for singles and pairs

COLLAR HARNESS FOR SINGLE TURNOUT

Using a full collar harness with a correctly fitting collar allows the best use to be made of the horse's 'pulling power'. Collar harness for a single turnout consists of a collar, a saddle or pad, the traces, and the hame tugs. The latter are short so that they remain in front of the shaft tugs. The collar is pear-shaped to give an anatomically correct fit around the shoulders and the chest. The collar should be sufficiently well padded to keep the hame tugs clear of the shoulders at all times, and so avoid chafing. The hames, which lie on top of the padded part of the collar, must be of the highest quality material because they have to take a great deal of strain. On single harness the hames are connected at their bottom end by a chain or link. At the top they are held together by the hame strap. The top of the collar is protected by a little leather 'cap' to prevent water penetrating the stuffing. On single harness the buckle of the hame strap points to the left, and the point of the strap to the right. As every driving person knows, this is so that the hame strap can easily be undone from the offside in an emergency. With pairs and multiples, the point of the hame strap always faces inwards, towards the opposite horse.

The hame tug is fixed to the hames by a non-detachable steel ring which passes through the hame draught eye. On the top third of the hames are the movable rein terrets. On pairs harness the rings should be movable, but on single harness they may be rigid.

The hame tug buckles at the end of the hame tugs should be as flat as possible, so as to allow maximum clearance between them and the shafts. The traces attach to the hame tug buckles. The length is adjusted by means of about five oval-shaped holes at the end of the traces, the third (middle) hole being about 25cm from the end of the trace.

At the rear end of each trace is a metal running loop (with a little leather tab or hand-piece) by which the trace is attached to the vehicle (to the swingle tree or splinter bar). *[In Britain, most single harness traces have a 'crew hole' at the end which fastens onto the trace hook on the end of the swingle tree – Translator.]*

The saddle or pad is constructed in the same way as for breastcollar harness and is judged by the same criteria. The same applies to the kicking strap or breeching.

COLLAR HARNESS FOR PAIRS

Full collar harness for pairs differs from single harness in the following respects:

- The hames are connected at the bottom by a 'kidney link' with a pole strap ring on it.

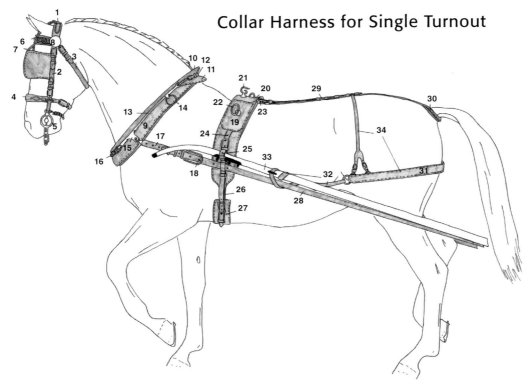

Collar Harness for Single Turnout

1. Headpiece with winker stay buckle
2. Cheekpiece with blinker and winker stay
3. Throatlatch or throatlash
4. Noseband
5. Bit with curb chain
6. Browband with chain or other decoration
7. Face drop
8. Rosette
9. Collar
10. Neck of collar
11. Protective cap
12. Hame strap
13. Hames
14. Movable terret
15. Hame draught eye
16. Chain fastener (or link)
17. Hame tug
18. Hame tug buckle
19. Saddle skirt
20. Saddle or pad
21. Bearing hook
22. Pad terret
23. 'D' for attachment of backstrap
24. Backband
25. Tug (metal 'Tilbury' tug for four-wheeled vehicle, leather 'open' pattern tug for two-wheeled vehicle)
26. Girth strap
27. Girth
28. Trace
29. Backstrap
30. Crupper dock piece (sewn on)
31. Breeching body
32. Breeching strap
33. Shaft
34. Breeching

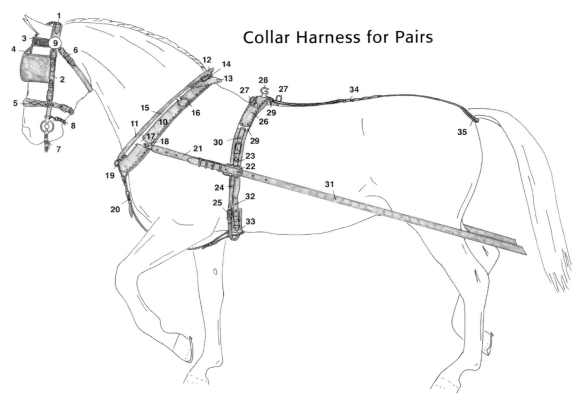

Collar Harness for Pairs

1. Headpiece with winker stay buckle
2. Cheekpiece with blinkers and winker stays
3. Browband with chain or other decoration
4. Face drop
5. Noseband with slots and keepers
6. Throatlatch or throat lash
7. Bit with curb hooks ('Liverpool' bit)
8. Curb chain with lip strap ring
9. Rosette
10. Collar
11. Rim of collar
12. Neck of collar
13. Protective cap
14. Hame strap
15. Hames
16. Movable (non-rigid) terret
17. Hame tug arm
18. Hame draught eye
19. Kidney link with ring
20. Breast plate or false martingale with drop
21. Hame tug
22. Tug buckle
23. Pad strap
24. False belly band point strap
25. False belly band
26. Pad
27. Rigid pad terret
28. Bearing hook
29. 'D's for attachment of backstrap and pad strap
30. Pad strap buckle attachment
31. Trace
32. Girth strap
33. Girth
34. Backstrap
35. Crupper dock piece (sewn on)

- The hame terrets should be movable (i.e. not rigid).

- The hame tugs attached to the hames are longer than those used for single harness, and the hame tug buckles have attachment points to which the tug strap, or pad strap, and the belly band or belly band point strap are sewn or buckled.

- The outside traces are 5cm longer than the inside ones for the same reason as with pairs breastcollar harness.

- There may be no rosette on the inside of the bridles.

The other parts, such as the backstrap, crupper, etc. work in the same way as with breastcollar harness.

Reins for single and pairs harness

For safety reasons, the way the reins are made is of paramount importance. They must be manufactured from the best quality materials, with no weak points and no dangerous design features. The safety of the reins must be maintained through constant, correct care, and by regular inspection. They should not be oiled: only products designed especially for reins should be used on them.

With pairs and teams the reins have an additional function: they are used by the driver to balance out the differences in the build and shape of the horses and to ensure that each horse does an equal share of the work.

When driving a pair, however good the reins, they will only serve their purpose if they are the correct length. They should therefore be checked from time to time for stretching or distortion.

> **Note**: To check the length of the reins, the coupling reins are buckled in the third hole (from the driver's end) on the draught reins. This is known as the 'check hole'; with the coupling reins in this position, the draught and coupling reins should be the same length. However, the length at the bit end (at the rein billets) must be the same on both reins.

The reins should be made out of natural, undyed leather.

SINGLE HARNESS REINS

The reins used with single harness consist of two separate pieces, each about 4.5m long, with a buckle fastening at one end to attach them to the bit, and another to connect them at the other end. The above measurement of 2 x 4.5m applies to a full-size horse and carriage.

With ponies or different types of vehicle the length of the reins varies accordingly. New reins should be about 27mm wide. With use they stretch and become narrower.

PAIR REINS

'Achenbach' reins consist of two full-length reins, known as 'draught reins', which are 4.5m in length, and two adjustable, crossed 'coupling reins' 3.02m in length. On the draught reins there are eleven oval holes, 4cm apart, to which the inside reins are buckled. They are oval so that the tongue of the coupling buckle lies flat, and to make it easier to adjust them.

The sixth hole, which is the basic setting (see p.57) for medium-sized horses, is 2.9m from the buckle at the bit end of the rein. The Achenbach reins fulfil all the requirements of pair reins. Their essential features are as follows:

- The rein billet has only one hole, and a long, easy to operate buckle. The single hole is to ensure that the adjustment of the coupling reins at the coupling buckles remains accurate. On the coupling rein, the bit buckle is sewn onto the flesh side of the leather so that when the rein is crossed over to the opposite horse it is the grain side which is uppermost and so visible to the onlooker.

- The keeper sewn onto the inside, coupling rein prevents the reins from separating too far up. Buckle guards underneath the coupling buckles serve to prevent the buckles damaging the reins and making unsightly marks on them.

- The buckle which connects the reins should be on the left one of the pair so that the driver will always know which is the right rein and which is the left.

This section would not be complete without a mention of the Viennese reins. Although with Viennese (Hungarian) reins there are more coupling holes, it is impossible to balance out different builds and temperaments in the horses with the same precision as with Achenbach reins. Many driving people consider the main advantage of Viennese or Hungarian reins to be that each horse can be driven with a separate rein.

Essential feature of Viennese or Hungarian reins are:

- Four holes on the rein billets. The two inside reins run through a metal or ivory ring.

- The coupling is in the driver's hand and is known as the 'frog'.

- On each of the four reins there are up to twenty adjustment holes, i.e. up to eighty in all.

Additional and auxiliary equipment

Described below are a few items of additional and auxiliary equipment and how they are used with singles and pairs. Although they are not part of the necessary equipment, and some are not permitted in public competitions, they can sometimes be helpful in training and everyday driving.

1. A curb guard made of rubber or leather, which is used to protect thin-skinned horses from chafing and pressure sores caused by the curb chain.

2. Ear covers, which serve to protect against flies, are permitted. 'Sallengs' should also be mentioned: these are artistically braided leather straps with long fringes, and are used with Hungarian harness for decoration and as a protection against flies.

3. Brushing boots protect the horse's fetlocks from injury, especially in cross-country and long-distance driving. Brushing, i.e. striking the foot against the opposite fetlock, is a common cause of injury, for example when the horse has just been fitted with new shoes. Brushing boots are permitted only in the marathon and obstacle-driving competitions. The same applies to overreach boots.

4. Heavily padded cruppers are designed to improve the tail carriage on horses which clamp their tails, and to prevent the reins being trapped underneath.

5. Bandages and boots protect the cannon bones and shins from external injury. They are not permitted in dressage competitions.

6. A flash noseband is a narrow strap threaded through a small loop sewn onto the front of the main noseband, and fastened around the jaw below the bit. When a flash noseband is used, the main noseband is passed through a special, flexible loop on the cheekpieces instead of being be rigidly anchored to them.

7. A puller strap is used with a horse which is heavy in hand to transfer part of the action of the bit onto the bottom of the nasal bone, and so is supposed to teach the horse not to pull. Puller straps are permissible for exercise and training.

flash noseband

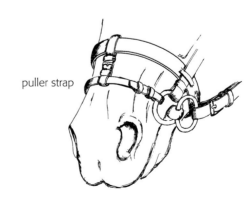

puller strap

CARE OF EQUIPMENT

Driving equipment is expensive and needs to be looked after. This includes cleaning it every time it is used. Leather parts should be wiped with a damp sponge or cloth to remove the dirt and then be cleaned again, with saddle soap.

Bits and metal parts or fittings should be wiped with a damp cloth or sponge. Every time the harness is cleaned, the condition of the stitching and the moving parts of the bit should be checked. Once the leather parts have been thoroughly cleaned they should be treated with grease or oil on the flesh side – the harness should, have course, have been completely taken apart beforehand. Leather parts which do not come into direct contact with the horse should have a thin layer of special leather dressing grease rubbed into them. However, grease should not be used on patent leather, which should be polished with a woollen cloth or cleaned with special patent leather cream. Leather parts which come in contact with the horse – for example, the inside of the collar or breastcollar – and the lining of the pad, should be treated with a leather dressing oil after cleaning. Leather needs moisture if it is to keep its firm, fibrous structure. The aim of oiling the leather is to keep it moist. Leather dressing oil keeps the leather supple, but if used in excess it softens the fibres and cause the leather to lose its firmness. A thin film of oil should be smeared over the buckles and metal parts. The metal fittings on the harness, such as the rosettes, can be cleaned and polished with metal polish. However, chemical cleaning products should not be used on bits. Any damaged stitching must be repaired immediately. Metal fittings with cracks or sharp edges – for example, slide-mouth bits – must be replaced straight away. Harness should be stored in a room which is dust-free and not too dry, and which can be heated in the winter. Harness should be hung on rounded wooden or metal brackets to prevent it splitting or cracking. Wet leather should be dried out in the open air, never in blazing sunshine or a hot oven.

PREPARATIONS FOR DRIVING

HORSE CARE

How the horse is kept, fed and cared for are important for its performance and well-being. Everyone involved with driving horses must have a basic knowledge of this subject.

Daily grooming serves to clean the dust and dirt from the hair and skin, along with waste products such as scurf and sweat. It also serves as a massage, stimulating the circulation in the skin and underlying connective tissue, and helping the skin to breathe. Hence grooming is not just a cleaning process, but is important for the horse's health and well-being.

In a **natural environment** horses perform this function by scratching and nibbling each other and themselves, and by rolling. In this situation, too much cleaning could be harmful, since a build-up of dust and grease protects the horse against the elements.

With a **stabled horse**, man must take over the responsibility for grooming. The **grooming kit** consists of a body brush, curry comb, dandy brush, linen or wool stable rubbers, sponges, a mane comb and a hoof pick. Electric grooming machines are a good investment, especially in larger establishments, since they save time and energy. Grooming can be done outside or in the corridor between the stables. **Tying** the horse 'pillar rein' style, with a rope on each side prevents misbehaviour. Quick-release knots or fastenings (for example, the so-called '**panic clips**'), should be used at both ends of the rope. They must be able to be released easily even when the rope is under tension, i.e. when the horse is pulling on it.

First the coat is thoroughly but carefully scuffed with the oval metal **curry comb**. *[This type of curry comb is in common use in continental Europe. It does not have 'teeth' like the square metal curry combs found in Britain, which must not be used on the horse – Translator.]* The curry comb is not used on the parts of the body where the bones or tendons lie directly underneath the skin (for example, the head, limbs and hips).

After the curry comb, the **body brush** is used to clean the skin, starting at the head and working in the direction of the hair. After each stroke the brush is passed over the curry comb, which is tapped on the ground from time to time to remove the dust which has built up in it. Finally the horse is wiped with a cloth ('stable rubber') to remove the last traces of dust from the skin.

The corners of the eyes, the nostrils, the sides of the mouth, the dock and the sheath should be cleaned with a **sponge** as necessary. Two different sponges should be used, one for the head and one for the dock and sheath. The sponges should be frequently and thoroughly washed in hot water.

After strenuous exercise, if the weather is favourable, the horse can be carefully washed down. Sponging down the parts which have been in contact with the harness is particularly beneficial and makes grooming easier.

The **tail** should be worked through with the fingers. It should not be combed or brushed since this pulls out too many hairs. The tail can be washed as necessary with warm water or with a suitable shampoo. The **mane** should be combed with a mane comb or brushed with a damp brush.

In normal circumstances, using **rugs** only serves to reduce the horse's resistance to colds. However, with horses which grow thick winter coats or sweat profusely when worked, it may be better to clip them and rug them up. Otherwise in cold, damp weather the coat takes a long time to dry out, which increases the risk of the horse catching cold.

HARNESSING UP, PUTTING TO AND TAKING OUT, UNHARNESSING

Putting the various items of harness and equipment on the horse is called harnessing up. This is usually done in the corridor between the stables. Immediately before putting the harness on, the horse should be brushed over to ensure it is clean. Small adhesions of straw or dung or encrusted hair or dirt in any form can cause pressure sores or chafing if part of the harness lies directly on top of them.

The harness is put on in the following order:

- The collar or breastcollar is put on.

- The saddle or pad is fitted.

- The pad strap is fastened to the tug buckle (on pairs harness) .

- The crupper is fitted

- The breast plate, or false martingale, is attached to the girth and the girth done up.

- The bridle is put on, and the throatlatch, noseband and curb chain are done up in that order.

- The reins are passed through the terrets and fastened to the bit (or the coupling rein to the throatlatch).

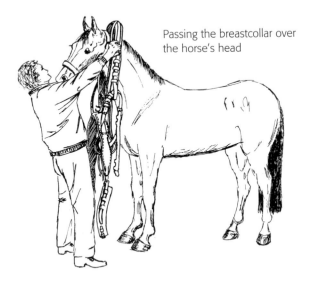

Passing the breastcollar over the horse's head

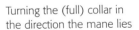

Turning the (full) collar in the direction the mane lies

Although sometimes inconvenient, it is a good idea to keep the horse tied up by the headcollar rope while it is being harnessed. This ensures that it stands quietly. Before harnessing up, the various parts of the harness should be sorted and set out ready. With young or fidgety horses, when putting on pairs harness, the collar or breastcollar, with the traces coiled up, can be unbuckled from the pad and put on separately. With older horses, which are used to the harness, collar and pad can stay buckled together.

The driver then places the pad on his left forearm (with pairs harness) and, holding the breastcollar by the sides, where the neckstrap is joined on, he slides it carefully over the horse's head without banging the horse's eyes (the headcollar rope is removed for this operation).

The breastcollar is then turned on the horse's neck, in the direction of the lie of the mane, and the pad placed on the back just behind the withers.

Full collar harness is put on in the same way except that the collar is held at the point where the hame tugs are attached to the hames, with the wide part of the collar uppermost, i.e. upside down. Next the collar is turned round the narrowest part of the horse's neck, in the direction of the lie of the mane, and slid back onto the shoulders. The pad is then placed on the back.

The false martingale should be held under one hand to prevent it getting in the way when the collar is being put on. On pairs harness, if the collar or breastcollar is not already joined to the pad, the pad strap should then be attached to the pad strap buckle attached to the 'D' on the tug buckle.

The next task is to put the crupper on. The tail is doubled over and passed through the dock piece of the crupper, which is held with the other hand. The dock piece is then pushed right up to the root of the tail and the hairs straightened and smoothed down. For safety reasons the driver should stand to one side of the horse's quarters. A crupper with a detachable dock piece can be very useful with young horses. Once the crupper is in place the pad can be put in the correct position just behind the withers and the false belly band loosely done up. The false martingale, which is buckled onto the collar, can then be attached to the girth.

To put on the bridle, the driver stands on the left side of the horse's head and, holding the headpiece of the bridle in his right hand, raises it level with the horse's forehead, taking care not to hit the horse in the eyes with the blinkers.

Then, holding the bit across its full width in his left hand, he pushes it into the horse's mouth and at the same time lifts the bridle up with his right hand. Once the headpiece is lying flat and in the correct position behind the horse's ears, the forelock can be straightened underneath the browband and face drop. The throatlatch is then fastened. There should be sufficient room between it and the throat when the head is flexed.

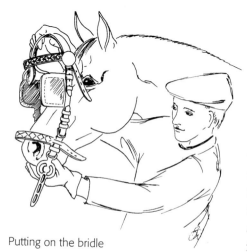
Putting on the bridle

34

Note: The throatlatch should be fastened first, then the noseband, and finally the curb chain.

Note: If the throatlatch is too loose, it makes it easier for the horse to get the bridle off. The throatlatch buckle, especially the outside one on pairs harness, should be level with the cheekpiece buckles. The height of the noseband should be such that it does not press on the corners of the mouth or rub the cheek bones. If the noseband is too loose, it will not do its job, which is to keep the cheekpieces and (curb) bit in position. If it is too tight it will restrict the action of the curb chain and cause the action of the bit to be transferred to the nose. If a flash attachment is used, the noseband is free to move through the cheekpieces, instead of being anchored to them, and is fastened more tightly. The noseband is done up before the flash strap. This prevents it being pulled downwards when the latter is fastened.

The bit should not pull the corners of the mouth upwards, nor should it hang down and rattle against the horse's teeth, especially the tushes in stallions and geldings. The width of the bit should match the width of the horse's mouth. Ports which are too high prevent the horse mouthing the bit. They do not give the horse a better contact or make it come onto the aids any more easily, and they often cause mouth injuries.

The upper cheeks of the bit should be angled outwards slightly so as not to rub the horse's cheeks. The length of the curb hooks should be such that the curb chain lies exactly in the curb groove. The opening on the curb hooks should be at the front to prevent the hook getting caught on the pole or on the adjacent horse. The curb chain should be turned clockwise until it is flat. The lip strap ring should be at the bottom. When the driver has a contact with the horse's mouth the cheek of the bit should be at an angle of no more than 30–45° to the horse's mouth.

Note: The curb chain must be correctly adjusted. If it is too loose the cheeks will 'bottom out' (angle too great), and if it is too short the bit will 'bind' (insufficient angle) or pinch the horse.

Finally the reins are threaded through the terrets. They should always lie flat with the grain side uppermost. The rein with the buckle on the rear end goes on the left, and the one without the buckle on the right. With single harness the reins are passed through the terrets on the pad and then those on the neckstrap.

The rein is fastened to the bit in whatever position is desired or necessary. If a mild action is required, on a double ring ('Wilson') snaffle the rein billet is buckled to both rings together.

With pairs the billet of the outside (draught) rein passes round the back part of the bit ring as well as the cheek of the bit. The inside (coupling) rein is attached only to the cheek, since otherwise the sideways pull of the rein would cause the bit to tilt and dig into the side of the mouth. With pairs, as with singles, the grain side of the leather should be uppermost, the rein with the buckle on the end goes on the left side, and the one without the buckle on the right. The left draught rein goes to the left horse and the coupling rein goes to the right horse; the right draught rein goes to the right horse and its coupling rein to the left horse. On correct pair breastcollar harness there are rein terrets on the neckstraps. Since when the horses are 'put to' the inside rein is crossed over to the opposite horse, when the harness is put on this rein is attached temporarily to the throatlatch by passing the end round the throatlatch and then from front to back through the keeper next to the buckle. The draught rein is attached to the bit immediately. The other ends (hand parts) of the reins, which with a pair have not yet been buckled together, are fastened to the pad terret to make sure they do not hang down and get caught up and broken when the horse is led to the vehicle. The traces are laid across the back under the backstrap.

> **Note**: When using breastcollar harness with pairs and teams, the reins should also be passed through the terrets on the neckstraps.

After harnessing up, the following points should be checked to ensure that the harness is correctly fitted:

- The breast piece of the breastcollar should be positioned about two fingers' breadth above the point of the shoulder. If it is fitted any lower it will restrict the movement of the horse's shoulders and forelegs and may cause galling and pain.

- On breastcollar harness the pole strap ring should be offset slightly towards the pole head. If it is offset to the outside, this means that the harnesses are the wrong way round, that is the left (nearside) set is on the right (offside) horse and vice versa.

- The neckstrap should be positioned on the horse's neck in the hollow just in front of the withers. From there it should slope forwards slightly to the point where it is attached to the breast piece. It should never slope backwards since this would make it press down hard on the neck and cause injury. The neckstrap is adjusted so that it supports the breast piece in the correct position. The pole is supported by the yoke strap.

- The saddle or pad should lie about 10cm behind the highest point of the withers, and the channel at the top should not touch the horse's back. If there is not enough room between the leather and the metal tree and the back, the pad needs to be restuffed. As a temporary measure a piece of foam rubber or some other kind of protective pad can be used underneath.

- The false belly band on pairs harness serves to support the traces, and so can be done up fairly loosely. The false belly band and the pad strap should be adjusted so that the line of draught between the hame draught eye and the swingle tree remains straight even when the horses are trotting at speed. As with the girth on pairs harness, the false belly band should fasten on the outside.

- To prevent the reins getting caught under them, the free ends of the straps on the backstrap should not protrude beyond the end of the last keeper. There should be sufficient slack in the backstrap to allow it to spring up and down slightly with the movement.

- The kicking strap on single harness passes through a loop on the backstrap. When attached to the shafts, the kicking strap runs behind the points of the hips and over the top of the croup.

- The kicking strap passes through the backstrap and runs obliquely behind the points of the hips to the attachment points on the shafts. It should not restrict the horse's action, but serve only to limit the upward movement. When the kicking strap is fastened to the vehicle, there should be enough room to insert a hand on its side between the strap and the horse's croup.

- If a breeching is used, the breeching body should be about a hand's breadth below the points of the buttocks. When the horse is stood up in its traces there should be room to insert a fist on each side underneath the breeching body below the points of the buttocks. The breeching straps should be adjusted so that there is sufficient room in the breeching: it must not pinch, or rub the hind legs. It also acts as a trace bearer, and as such should not break the line of draught.

- A full collar should be well stuffed, and the shape should be anatomically correct: that is it should be pear-shaped, and not egg-shaped, so that it matches the shape of the horse's neck. The collar should have as large a bearing surface as possible, but should leave the joints and the windpipe free. If it fits correctly you should be able to run the tip of a finger down either side between the collar and the horse's neck, and there should be room at the bottom to insert a fist between the collar and the windpipe. If the collar is too long, a wedge-shaped pad in the top may bring about some improvement. The sides of the collar should be sufficiently well padded to prevent the hame tugs rubbing against the horse in any circumstances. The hame strap should point to the inside (or on single harness to the right) to make it easier to undo the hames if the horse falls. The false martingale, which passes through the kidney link and round the collar, attaches to the girth and helps to keep the collar in position against the horse's breast, for example when halting or reining back.

Note: Buckles, on all parts of the harness, should be done up tightly enough to secure the harness, but not so tightly that it restricts the horse's movements or breathing, or causes pain, pressure or chafing.

Putting to

SINGLE TURNOUT

To do this correctly, the vehicle must first be positioned where it is safe for horses and handlers. The whip should be in the socket. In order to prevent trouble from the outset, an assistant should be available to supervise the horse throughout the process. If the driver does have to put the horse to on his own, he must keep hold of the reins at all times.

To put the horse to, it is led, ready harnessed, to the vehicle, and positioned so that it is facing in the same direction as the vehicle. An assistant lifts up the shafts approximately to breast height and pushes the vehicle up to the horse so that it is standing between the shafts. If the driver is alone, he should back the horse into the shafts. Obviously this method is not to be recommended, especially with young or inexperienced horses. Once the horse is between the shafts the assistant stands in front of it and ensures that it does not step forwards.

The harness is attached to the vehicle as follows:

- The shafts are placed in the tugs. The belly band is then done up first on the nearside (left) and then on the offside (right). *[This is the method used with Tilbury tugs, i.e. on a four-wheeled vehicle. With a two-wheeled vehicle, open pattern tugs are used. The shafts are pushed through the tugs as far as the tug stops, and the belly band fastened on the nearside.]*

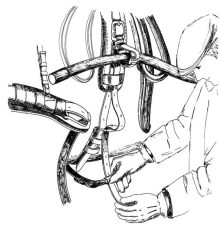

Fastening the belly band, with Tilbury tugs

- The traces are attached, the right one first, by slipping the leather loops* on the end onto the swingle tree, or possibly to the splinter bar if full collar harness is used. The quick-release tab on the trace end should point to the rear. [* *In Britain, most swingle trees, especially those used with single turnout, are equipped with trace hooks, and the traces have a 'crew hole' at the end to attach them to the hook – Translator.*]

- The kicking strap is attached to and around the shaft, with the trace running through the loop between it and the shaft, so that it also acts as a trace bearer.

- When the horse has been put to, the driver checks every detail again, paying particular attention to the length of the traces. If, when the horse is stood up in its traces, the shaft tug is pushed forward, this means the traces are too short. If the tip of the shaft is level with the back of the shoulder blade the traces are too long.

PAIRS

For driving on the right-hand side of the road, the steadier horse is normally placed on the left because this is the traffic side. When putting to a pair, an assistant should always be available. Only when absolutely quiet, very experienced horses are being used can the driver do the job on his own. The horses are led up to the vehicle and positioned alongside the pole. Care should be taken because the horses cannot see around them because of the blinkers, and can bump into door frames, the vehicle or the pole.

The horses are put to as follows:

- The coupling reins are attached. The rein of the horse with the higher head carriage is placed on top. The reins are turned so that the grain side is uppermost.

- The end of the right rein is removed from the terret of the right (offside) horse and thrown over the horses' backs to the left side.

- The pole straps (or pole chains) are passed though the kidney link rings from the inside to the outside, and loosely fastened.

- The ends of the reins are buckled together and tucked from behind under the pad strap, so that the hand parts are pointing to the rear and so are readily accessible.

- The right outside trace, and then the right inside one are attached to the swingle tree, or (alternatively, with full collar harness) to the splinter bar. The outside trace is attached first to prevent the horse stepping sideways.

- The left horse's traces are attached in the same order – first the outside then the inside one.

- The length of the pole straps or chains is adjusted to provide a taut but springy connection between the pole head and the kidney link ring – they should not be so tight that the collars or breastcollars are pulled forward.

Different types of attachment

pole

swingle tree

swingle bar

splinter bar — pole pin

quick-release tab

roller bolt

trace

pole head

pole head

1. Swingle trees on a swingle bar
(fully articulated attachment)

2. Splinter bar
(rigid attachment)

3. Swingle trees on a fixed bar
(semi-rigid attachment)

The outside horse brings the vehicle into the turn by pushing the pole in the new direction with its shoulder. Less precision is possible than with a splinter bar or swingle trees attached to a splinter bar. Forward-going horses are required, otherwise you tend to get a 'see-sawing' effect. Because the angle of the swingle bar to which the horses are attached is constant, although adjusting the coupling reins will compensate for differences in build or conformation, it will not balance out different temperaments or help to make the horses work equally. This type of attachment is seen mainly with agricultural vehicles and implements, though recently a cross between this system and the semi-rigid system has appeared on marathon vehicles. This system can be used with breastcollar or full collar harness.

The outside horse brings the vehicle into the turn by pulling harder. This system makes it possible to drive very precisely. Forward-going, experienced horses are required because there is no 'give' in this type of attachment. It is possible, by adjusting the coupling reins, to compensate or correct for different temperaments and unequal distribution of the work, as well as different builds. In Germany, splinter bars are rarely used. They are seen mostly on heavy English carriages. They should not be used with breastcollar harness since they tend to make the collar rub the shoulders.

The outside horse brings the vehicle into the turn by pulling harder. This is the system which permits the greatest precision. It is also ideal for bringing on young horses. It is possible, by adjusting the coupling reins, to compensate or correct for different temperaments and unequal distribution of the work, as well as different builds. Swingle trees on a fixed bar are the most widely used form of attachment, and can be used with either full collar or breastcollar harness.

- The last task is to perform a final check of all the harness and attachments. The girths should be tightened to keep the pads firmly in place. The assistant should remain standing in front of the horses while they are being put to. On safety grounds he should stand to one side of the pole head, and he may need to hold the reins rather than the cheekpieces. If the driver has no alternative but to put the horses in by himself, he should stand them facing away from the stable or facing a wall. He should attach the coupling reins and buckle the reins together before leading the horses to the vehicle, and should be sure to keep hold of the end of the reins. This is tedious, but necessary on safety grounds. After a final check to ensure that the horses have been put in correctly and everything is in order, the reins can be taken up and the driver and passengers can mount.

Taking out

Both singles and pairs are taken out in the opposite order to that in which they are put to. Whatever operation is being performed, the first priority is always safety. The brake is applied before the driver gets down, and the whip is placed in the socket. The driver keeps hold of the reins. With an assistant standing in front of the horse, the first task is to undo the kicking strap from the shafts. Then the traces are unhooked and placed on the horse's back underneath the crupper. Next the shafts are released from the tugs and put down carefully on the ground, and the reins are fastened to the terret. The horse is then led forward out of the shafts.

With pairs the procedure is basically the same as for putting to, but in the reverse order:

- The right horse's traces are unhooked, inside trace first, and placed on the back under the crupper.

- The left horse's traces are unhooked, inside trace first, and placed on the back under the crupper.

- The pole straps or chains are undone and placed on top of the pole.

- The reins are unbuckled from each other and the rear end of the left rein is fastened to the nearside terret. The driver then goes to the other side and fastens the rear end of right rein to the offside horse's right terret.

- The inside reins are unfastened from the bits and attached to the throatlatch of the horse opposite by passing the point round and back through the keeper.

- The horses are led away from the vehicle at a slight angle.

Unharnessing

After the horses have been taken out of the vehicle they are unharnessed in the reverse order to harnessing up:

- The reins are unfastened and pulled out through the terrets.

- The bridle is removed. It should be undone in the following order: first the curb chain, then the noseband, and then the throatlatch. Finally the headcollar is put on.

- The horse may be tied up to facilitate the rest of the operation.

- The traces are coiled up.

- The girth is undone.

- The crupper is removed.

- The saddle or pad is removed and placed on the left forearm.

- The collar or breastcollar is removed. The horse is first untied, then the collar is turned upside down at the thinnest part of the horse's neck, grasped on both sides, and carefully slid over the horse's head.

- The horse is tied up.

It goes without saying that the horse should be cleaned down before it is put away, and the harness should be hung up tidily for cleaning. The horse should also be checked for injuries or loose shoes.

THE VEHICLE AND ITS CARE

Types of vehicle

The vehicles in use today all belong to the following groups: phaeton, dog-cart, gig, '*jagdwagen*' (hunting phaeton, Beaufort phaeton), brake, wagonette and modern competition vehicle (marathon vehicle). There are many other vehicles with different names (some purely fanciful) but they can all be traced back to these basic types.

With any vehicle, the points to be taken into consideration are:

- Stability

- Weight

- Manoeuvrability

- Free running qualities (minimum rolling resistance)

- Safety

The vehicle must also do the job and be suited to the kind of turnout for which it is intended – for example, the phaeton is a pair or team vehicle, a dog-cart is for single turnout, and a brake is essentially a team vehicle. Good vehicles can be bought to order from a number of specialised firms. Unfortunately there are also some impractical and often very unattractive vehicles on the market. For competitions, especially international ones, set weights and widths are laid down for the vehicle in certain disciplines, such as horse driving trials. Details of these are set out in the national rules for each country (in Germany the *LPO* or *Leistungs-Prüfungs-Ordnung*) and in the rules of the *Fédération Équestre Internationale*. Also, a basic knowledge of vehicle construction and the design of the different parts is important for anyone involved in driving.

Operational Safety Considerations

The technical aspects of vehicle and harness safety are of the utmost importance. Information on this subject (in German) can be found in the following publications:

(a) *Richtlinien für den Bau und Betrieb pferdebespannter Fahrzeuge* (Principles of Building and Operating Horse-drawn Vehicles) published by the Deutsche Reiterlichen Vereinigung e.V., with the approval of DEKRA AG and the *Verband der Technischen Überwachungsvereine e.V. (VdTÜV)*,

(b) *Sicherheitstechnische Bewertung von Pferde- und Ponygeschirren – FN- Empfehlungen für mehr Sicherheit im Strassenverkehr* (Safety Considerations in Horse and Pony Harness – Recommendations for Greater Safety when Driving on the Roads).

> **Note**: These guidelines are based on recognised principles and reflect modern technology. They have liability and insurance implications and should therefore be respected at all costs.

THE GERMAN ROAD TRAFFIC ACT (*STRASSENVERKEHRSORDNUNG*)
Para 1 Basic rules
(1) Driving in traffic requires constant vigilance and mutual consideration.
(2) Every road user must conduct himself so as not to injure or endanger any other road user, or obstruct or inconvenience him except insofar as is unavoidable.

THE GERMAN RULES ON VEHICLE CONSTRUCTION AND USE
(*STRASSENVERKEHRS-ZULASSUNGS-ORDNUNG*)
Para 30 Vehicle construction
(1) Vehicles should be constructed and equipped in such a way that

    1. Their operation on the roads does not injure or endanger any other road

user, or obstruct or inconvenience him except insofar as is unavoidable.

2. The occupants are protected as far as possible from injury, especially in the case of accident, and the extent and consequences of any injuries are minimised.

Para 31 Responsibility for the operation of vehicles

(1) Anyone who drives a vehicle, or interconnected vehicles, must be suitable for the purpose.

(2) The keeper shall not order or permit the operation if he is aware that the driver is unsuited to the purpose or the vehicle, interconnected vehicles, turnout, or load or contents is not correct, or that the load or contents have an adverse effect on the vehicle's safety in traffic.

> **Note**: The leaflet, in German, *Richtlinien für den Bau und Betrieb pferdebespannter Fahrzeuge* (Principles of Building and Operating Horse-drawn Vehicles) can be obtained free of charge from the Deutsche Reiterlichen Vereinigung e.V. (FN), 48229 Warendorf, Tel: (00 49 25 81) 63 62-222).

The wheels

Carriage wheels consist of a hub (nave), spokes and a rim (with an iron or rubber tyre). The construction of the wheels has a considerable effect on the efficiency: the larger the wheel, the more freely the vehicle runs. Small wheels cause a lot of resistance, especially on uneven ground and across country.

Nowadays, the wheel hub usually contains a grease-filled tapered roller bearing. The hubs are attached to the axle and, because of the friction caused by the wheel turning, the grease or oil needs to be checked frequently.

The axle arms slope downwards slightly so as to place as little strain as possible on the outside attachment of the wheel to the axle when the wheel is moving, and to direct the centrifugal force inwards to the middle of the axle.

To ensure that the oblique setting of the wheels does not cause the tyres to come in contact with the ground on the outside only, the spokes are attached to the hub at an angle, so that they slope outwards slightly: the wheels are said to be 'dished'. Dishing the wheels also has the advantage that the dirt picked up by the moving wheels is thrown outwards.

The running surfaces of wooden wheels are normally protected by an iron rim and a solid rubber tyre. The front wheels should have the same track width as the rear ones. A wide track increases the stability of the vehicle. For competition driving, the

Dished wheel, angled outwards at the top (positive camber)

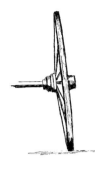

Dished wheel, angled inwards at the top (negative camber). Seen on marathon vehicles

maximum track width allowed is 1.6m. Marathon vehicles must have a track width of at least 1.25m. *[These rules may vary from country to country – Translator.]*

Shafts and pole

The **shafts** are two slightly bent wooden or metal poles attached directly to the splinter bar. The shafts must be far enough apart to allow the horse sufficient freedom of movement. The tips of the shafts should point outwards.

On the front third of each shaft, on the side, is a hook-shaped projection called a **tug stop**, against which the shaft tug rests. Bolts with prominent heads are unsuitable for this purpose since they do not fulfil the safety requirements.

Also for safety reasons, tug stops should be made of best quality materials since they are often the only means of stopping the vehicle or holding it back.

A 'D' is screwed onto the rear third of the shaft for the attachment of the kicking strap. There may also be another 'D' slightly in front of it for a breeching strap if required. Depending on the design of the vehicle, the shafts may be either removable or attached permanently. Attached to the splinter bar at the base of the shafts is the swingle tree.

The **swingle tree** serves as the point of attachment for the traces. It is hinged and free-moving. For horses, the minimum width of the swingle tree should be 65cm.

On the splinter bar are the **roller bolts**, to which the traces may be attached provided full collar harness is used. This form of attachment is not practical with single turnout. The heads of the roller bolts are 5–8cm in diameter and are situated on the left and right sides of the splinter bar, as close to the ends (and so as far apart) as possible.

A pole is used when the vehicle is pulled by two horses harnessed abreast. It serves to steer the vehicle, to stop it or hold it back (i.e. for braking) and, where applicable, to attach the equipment required for additional horses (main bar and lead bars for a four-in-hand and swing pole for a six-in-hand).

The **pole** should be made of wood (oak or birch) or metal. The end of the pole should be approximately in line with the horses' foreheads and level with the shoulder

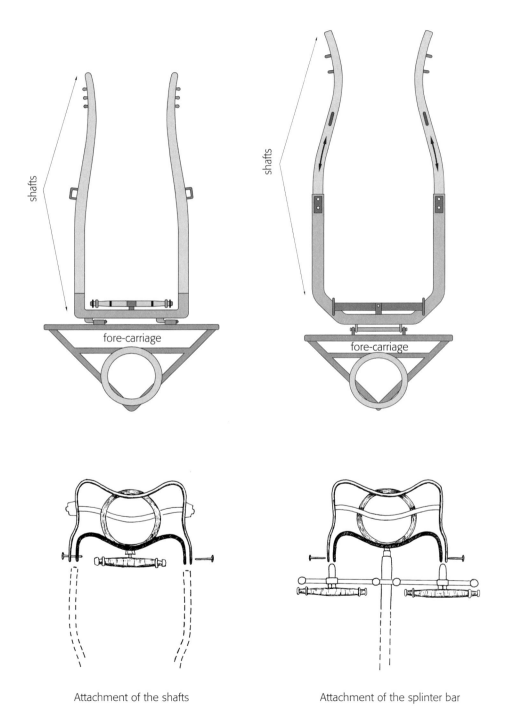

Attachment of the shafts

Attachment of the splinter bar

joints when the horses are stood up in their traces. At the front end of the pole is the **pole head**, to which the pole straps are attached. Because of the strain placed on it when holding the vehicle back (braking), the pole head must be made of the best quality materials. Pole heads on vehicles used for team driving are equipped with a **crab** for the attachment of the main bar. A strap is fitted across the gap between the end of the crab and the pole to prevent the bits or the harness of the wheelers from getting caught on it. The rear of the pole fits into a socket underneath the turntable. Slightly forward of this position, underneath the splinter bar, the pole passes through a steel bracket, where it is secured with a **pole pin** or **lynch pin**.

Brakes

A brake is essential to prevent undue strain on the horses *[refers to a four-wheeled vehicle – Translator]*. Frequent, correct use of the brake is the hallmark of a good driver. A bad driver lets the horses hold the vehicle back with the pole straps, or even lets it run into the backs of their hocks.

There are several different types of brakes:

- the wind-on brake (spindle brake),

- the push-on brake,

- the pull-on brake,

all of which are hand-operated, and

- the foot brake.

Wind-on (spindle) brake

Disc brake

The hand-operated brakes are located on the right-hand side of the vehicle, next to the driver's seat. The wind-on brake, which is the one which is best for hilly areas, is operated either by a wheel or a crank.

The push-on and pull-on brakes are operated by a lever and ratchet assembly positioned on the right, next to the driver's seat within reach of his hand. The pull-on variety is definitely preferable because the driver moves his body and left hand backwards when operating it. When using a push-on brake the upper body tips forward and the left hand goes forward with it, so that the horses actually lengthen their stride just as the brake is being applied.

The braking action is usually brought about by wooden or solid rubber brake blocks acting on the outside of the tyre, or by disc brakes. On pneumatic-tyred vehicles, braking is by means of brake drums inside the hubs.

With a foot brake, the pedal is on the footboard, and must be within easy reach of the driver's right or left foot. The foot brake has the advantage that it leaves the driver's hands free for handling the reins and giving traffic signals.

Vehicles with a foot brake must also have a hand-operated parking brake. All brakes should operate as quietly as possible. Brake blocks made of hornbeam, willow, poplar or lime wood are good because they do not make much noise. The mechanical parts of the brakes must be adequately greased, but the driver must ensure that any surplus grease is wiped off immediately so that he or his passengers do not get it on their clothes.

Foot brake

Lighting

[Regulations may vary from country to country – Translator.]
In common with all other vehicles travelling on public roads, a horse-drawn vehicle must be fitted with a functional lighting system. The legal requirement is for at least one white light showing to the front and at least one red light showing to the rear. The bottom of the light must not be lower than 0.6m and the top not higher than 1.55m from the ground.

The method of lighting – candle, battery or dynamo – is optional. For competitions it is stylish to have a carriage lamp with a candle on either side of the vehicle at the front.

Also required by law are two red reflectors on the back of the vehicle. The tops of the reflectors should not be more than 0.9m above the road surface.

Both the lights and the reflectors on the back should be as close as possible to the outside edges of the vehicle. In no circumstances should the light source or the reflector be more than 0.4m inboard from the widest point of the vehicle.

On each of the long sides of the vehicle there should be a yellow reflector every 2 metres. It should not be more than 0.6m from the road surface. On safety grounds these yellow reflectors should be fitted even on antique carriages and exercise carts since they are often used in the evenings, at dusk and after dark. Reflectors used on horse-drawn vehicles should be round.

The driver is responsible for ensuring that the lighting is in working order, clean and not obscured, for example by blankets etc. or by a passenger.

REQUIRED EQUIPMENT FOR SPORT, COMPETITIONS AND PLEASURE DRIVING
Vehicles must be constructed and equipped in such a way that their use on the roads does not injure or endanger any other road user, or obstruct or inconvenience him except insofar as is unavoidable, and that the occupants are protected as far as possible from injury, especially in the event of an accident, and the extent and consequences of any injuries are minimised (Para 30 StVZO).

- Vehicles must be constructed and maintained in such a way that they do not cause undue wear and tear on the road. For safety reasons (operational and safety in traffic), all important parts which wear out quickly or are easily damaged must be easy to inspect and replace.

- Safe and secure seats with side and rear supports must be provided for the driver and passengers.

- The design of the vehicle must be such that the driver and passengers can get on and off safely (Para 35d StVO). For safety reasons, the use of the hub of the vehicle as a step is not permitted. A step (not higher than 40cm) must be available.

Vehicle safety in traffic

Vehicle lighting

Reflective clothing for
increased safety

- The pole is held in place by the pole-pin or lynch-pin, which is secured with a split
  pin.

- The vehicle must be easy to steer (Para 64 (1) StVZO).

- Martingales *[referring to standing martingales, which in Germany are attached to the
  bit-rings – Translator]* are not permitted (Para 64 (2) StVZO).

- An adequate brake must be provided. It must be easy to use during the journey, and
  its use must not damage the road surface. An adequate brake is one which is perma-

nently affixed to the vehicle and which makes it possible to reduce the speed and bring the vehicle to a halt.

- At dusk, after dark, or at other times when required on safety grounds, there must be at least one white light showing to the front and at least one red light showing to the rear. These must be not more than 150cm above the road surface and not more than 40cm inboard from the widest point on the vehicle (including the splinter bar). They must not be dazzling. If a pair of lights is used, they must be equal and positioned at the same height (Para 66a StVZO).

- There must be two rear-facing red reflectors, which should be no higher than 90cm and no more than 40cm inboard from the widest point on the vehicle.

- Also required are two yellow reflectors, which should be no higher than 60cm. These must not be triangular (Para 66 (4) StVZO).

- It is advisable to have a forward-facing white reflector on the pole and on each side of the vehicle.

2

Basic Training of the Driver

Planning the training

Driving training is divided into the following sections:

- theoretical
- theoretical-cum-practical, and
- practical only

In the theoretical section the student is acquainted with the principles of the Achenbach system of driving, theoretical horse knowledge, traffic regulations, animal protection regulations and other legislation. This part of the training should be conducted in a classroom or, if the weather is suitable, outside in a quiet place where there is nothing to disturb the student's concentration. The theoretical-cum-practical training comprises the following: harness (including fitting, adjusting, harnessing and unharnessing), grooming and horse management, the driver's position, handling the reins (using the 'driving apparatus') and the application of the aids. Practical demonstration is an essential part of this training. Classrooms, harness rooms and the corridor between the stables can be used for this purpose. Training on the 'driving apparatus' should be carried out in manageable groups of up to four students.

When the student has mastered the necessary rein-handling techniques the training on the carriage can begin, along lanes and in open spaces where there is little or no traffic. An area used specially for driving training should be spacious, level and have a good surface, and there should be facilities for simulating various traffic situations. Only when the student is proficient in handling the turnout should training in traffic be introduced. Since the driving training is always carried out in walk to start with, the instructor should take over from time to time and drive the horses, mostly in trot, to prevent them 'going to sleep' and becoming 'sloppy' or getting impatient. In each section of the training the theoretical and the practical work should be alternated so as to retain the student's interest and not overtax him in any sphere.

TEACHING AND LEARNING AIDS FOR DRIVING INSTRUCTION

Teaching and learning aids

- manual containing the principles of driving, specialist literature
- blackboard, chalk, flipchart
- wallcharts
- projector
- overhead projector
- films
- audio cassettes
- videos
- loud hailer
- radio/cassette-players

Teaching materials

- horses ('partners')
- carriages
- harness
- reins
- models
- 'driving apparatus' ('simulator')
- 'wooden reins'

CONSTRUCTION AND USE OF THE DRIVING APPARATUS

The driving apparatus is the 'simulator' used for teaching the student how to hold and handle the reins, and for developing the correct muscles. It allows several students

'Driving apparatus'

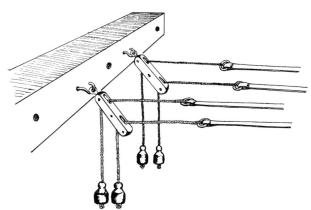

simultaneously to receive a thorough training without upsetting any horses' mouths. When learning the correct position of the hands and how to hold the whip, the student should wear gloves from the outset and carry a stick as a substitute for a whip. Holding the reins correctly is uncomfortable for the student to start with. Just as the person learning to ride finds that his 'riding muscles' ache, the driver has to contend with pains in his hands and forearms to start with.

A driving apparatus can be made cheaply, and is easily transported to the place where it is required. It is a good idea to construct it so that it can be used later for teaching students to handle team reins. Two metal or plastic pulleys each about 2–3cm in diameter are screwed or pinned into square holes cut into a square-section piece of hardwood about 20cm in length. A piece of cord about 60cm long is threaded through each pulley and a weight (about 1 kg) is attached to one end of each cord. An ordinary riding rein is attached to the other end. A team driving apparatus consists of two blocks of wood, each containing two pulleys. The blocks of wood are mounted on a wall or, better, on the edge of a table in such a way that they can move. They should be about 50cm above the ground and about 40–50cm apart. For teaching pair driving, only the bottom ('wheeler') reins are used.

The principles of the Achenbach system of driving

The seven principles of the Achenbach system of driving

1. For correct driving, Achenbach reins, a whip and a fixed splinter bar *[with or without swingle trees – Translator]* are required. If the bar is not fixed, the benefits of the Achenbach reins are lost.

2. Driving teams and multiples is based on single and pair driving. It is not necessary to 'convert', since in all cases the reins are held basically in the left hand.

3. The right hand must be available at any time to salute, use the brake or whip, or give traffic signals.

4. All turns are entered simply by yielding the outside rein. The stride is shortened just before the turn. Yielding the outside rein makes it easier for the outside horse to pull the vehicle into the turn. It also enables the horses to flex and bend in the direction of the movement. Keeping the backs of both hands vertical at all times makes it possible to turn the horses simply by turning the wrist.

- Right and left turns are fundamentally different, and so are driven in a different way. This is because the driver sits on the right (see 'Turns').

- Allowing one or more of the reins to slip through the hands makes it impossible to drive correctly and is dangerous in traffic and therefore unacceptable.

Holding and using the Achenbach 'crossed' reins

For Achenbach pair reins to be used correctly, the measurements must be correct. Only then will the full benefit be gained from the system. The horses should share the work equally and should be straight. The driver can tell if the horses are pulling equally by the traces (provided a fixed splinter bar is used of course), and by the pole, which should point straight ahead and be equidistant between the two horses. If the horses are not working equally the pole will always point sideways, towards the lazy horse.

If, when the driver has a contact on the reins, the horses' heads are permanently turned outwards, the coupling reins are too long. If the horses' heads are permanently turned inwards, the coupling reins are too short. However, the position of the reins should always be checked first – they may have been run through the terrets wrongly. Also check that the draught rein is on the outside.

If the horses are of normal height and more or less equal in temperament and build, both coupling reins should be done up on the sixth hole (counting from the driver's hand). This means that the coupling reins are set 12cm longer than the draught reins to make up for the extra distance they have to travel to the opposite horse's mouth. This setting is the normal setting (basic setting).

If the horses are very broad, the coupling rein has even further to travel because the horses' backs, and so the pad terrets, are further apart. To compensate for this the coupling reins should be fastened on the seventh, or even if necessary on the eighth hole (always counting from the driver's hand).

With narrow horses the inside reins have less distance to travel, so the coupling reins are fastened on the fifth or fourth hole, i.e. the basic setting is different.

In the basic setting, which is used when driving two horses of similar size, temperament and build, there is the same number of holes on each rein between the driver's hand and the coupling buckles.

However, the basic settings vary:

- Basic setting for medium-sized horses: sixth hole, with a total of ten holes showing between the driver's hand and the coupling buckles.

- Basic setting for large, broad horses: seventh or eighth hole, with a total of twelve holes showing between the driver's hand and the coupling buckles.

- Basic setting for small, narrow horses: fifth or fourth hole, with a total of eight holes showing between the driver's hand and the coupling buckles.

If the temperaments of the horses are different, the coupling rein to the more forward-going horse is fastened shorter than in the basic setting, and that of the less active horse is lengthened by the same amount, so that the total number of holes between the hand and the buckles is the same as in the basic setting.

EXAMPLE
The left horse of the pair is livelier, the right horse's traces are slacker than those of the left, and the pole points permanently to the right.

Correction
First the coupling rein to the left horse (buckle on the right rein) is shortened. The coupling rein to the right horse is lengthened by the same amount that the other side was shortened. This means that there are still ten holes in total between the hand and the buckles. Since after the adjustment the horses' heads point sideways, the driver must then shorten the rein through his hand (in this example the left rein) by the same amount that he has shortened or lengthened it at the buckle.

Holding the reins: single harness and pairs

The reins are held in the same way for both singles and pairs. The basic rules, according to the Achenbach system, are as follows:

- Both reins are held permanently in the left hand and secured by the bottom three fingers. The reins are separated by the index finger and the middle finger of the left hand. The left rein lies on top of the index finger and the right rein under the middle finger ('basic position').

- Both hands are involved in handling the reins, unless the right hand is required for

Achenbach reins

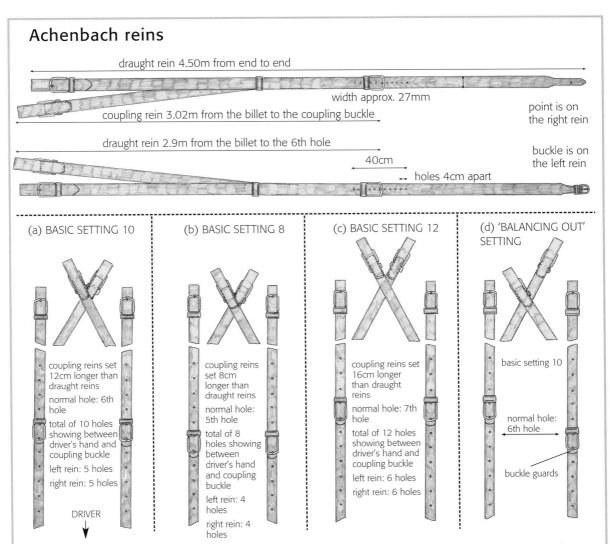

draught rein 4.50m from end to end

width approx. 27mm

coupling rein 3.02m from the billet to the coupling buckle

point is on the right rein

draught rein 2.9m from the billet to the 6th hole

40cm

buckle is on the left rein

holes 4cm apart

(a) BASIC SETTING 10

coupling reins set 12cm longer than draught reins

normal hole: 6th hole

total of 10 holes showing between driver's hand and coupling buckle

left rein: 5 holes

right rein: 5 holes

DRIVER

(b) BASIC SETTING 8

coupling reins set 8cm longer than draught reins

normal hole: 5th hole

total of 8 holes showing between driver's hand and coupling buckle

left rein: 4 holes

right rein: 4 holes

(c) BASIC SETTING 12

coupling reins set 16cm longer than draught reins

normal hole: 7th hole

total of 12 holes showing between driver's hand and coupling buckle

left rein: 6 holes

right rein: 6 holes

(d) 'BALANCING OUT' SETTING

basic setting 10

normal hole: 6th hole

buckle guards

ADJUSTING THE COUPLINGS TO COMPENSATE OR CORRECT FOR:

- different builds

- different temperaments

- unequal distribution of the work

(a) shows **basic setting 10** (i.e. a total of ten holes showing between the driver's hand and the coupling buckles) before the adjustment is been made to accommodate different builds or temperaments or to correct for unequal distribution of work:

To compensate for different builds – in (d) the reins are still at basic setting 10 (total of 10 holes between hand and buckles). However, here the right horse is essentially bigger (longer and

wider) than the left. The left coupling rein has therefore been lengthened and the right coupling rein shortened. This should cause both horses to look straight ahead. If this adjustment is insufficient, the left coupling rein should be lengthened by one more hole and the right one shortened by the same amount.

Important: The basic setting, i.e. the total number of holes between hand and coupling buckles, should remain the same, i.e. in this example, (d), the basic setting is still 10.

Note: For example, to bring the right horse further back, you fasten the coupling buckle closer to your hand on the left draught rein and further away by the same amount on the right rein.

another purpose, such as using the brake or the whip.

- A rein should never be allowed to slip through the fingers. The reins should be shortened or lengthened only by the prescribed methods.

- Only the horses are halted by the reins. The vehicle is stopped by the brake *[refers to a four-wheeled vehicle – Translator]*. Insufficient use of the brake causes the horses' mouths to become hard and insensitive.

- All turns are performed by yielding the outside rein, not pulling the inside one.

- When using the whip the driver must make absolutely sure that he does not disturb the horses in their mouths.

- When using the right hand to operate the hand brake, the whip must first be transferred to the left hand so that it does not touch the horse accidentally.

- Pulling and jerking the reins, which tends to be the layman's method of sending the horses forward, must be avoided. No one who persists in this practice will make a good driver.

- If a dangerous situation arises unexpectedly, any method of handling the reins may be adopted for the purpose of preventing an accident.

Note

Contact – the hand maintains a secure, steady, soft contact with the horse's mouth.

Length of reins – appropriate to the horse's length of frame, which is determined by the gait, the length of stride and how hard the horse is pulling.

Turns – first yield, then 'ask'; the outside rein leads the horse into and regulates the turn;
– the inside rein flexes the horse in the direction of the movement.

There are three different positions for holding the reins:

- the basic position

- the standard position

- the schooling position

The basic position

The basic position forms the basis for driving singles and pairs. It also serves as foundation for the position used for four-in-hand and six-in-hand driving. The two reins lie flat, grain side uppermost, in the left hand, with the right rein between the middle and third fingers and the left rein on top of the index finger. The bottom three fingers (middle, third and little fingers) grip the reins. The left hand is positioned in front of the middle of the abdomen in such a way that the driver can give and take in equal measure. The elbow lies without stiffness against the body. The back of the hand is vertical, and the hand is bent inwards slightly from the wrist. The right hand holds the whip and is positioned in front and half to the right of the left hand and at the same height.

About 10cm of the hand part of the whip protrudes below the hand, and the whip points forwards/upwards to the left.

Driving with the reins in this position must become second nature so that the driver will experience no difficulties later on when he comes to drive teams and multiples.

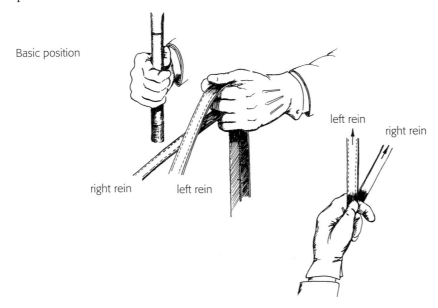

Basic position

right rein   left rein

left rein   right rein

The standard position

The standard position is the starting point for all subsequent rein handling techniques. It also takes some of the strain off the left hand on long journeys. In the standard position the left hand is held steady, as in the basic position. The right hand is placed on top of the right rein in front of the left hand so that the thumb and the right index finger is hooked over the left rein and the three lower fingers over the right rein, with the

Standard position

Schooling position (dressage position)

left rein

right rein

right rein   left rein

fingertips in contact with the underside (flesh side) of the reins. The whip is held by the thumb and index finger of the right hand. If the hand position is correct the whip, held at its point of balance (usually marked by a metal ring) maintains the correct position of its own accord, i.e. it points forwards and upwards to the left.

As in the other positions, the left hand remains in the basic position described earlier and keeps a firm hold of the reins – a rein must never be allowed to slip. On long journeys the fingers of the left hand may be opened and moved a little to prevent them becoming tired, but in this case the right hand should grip both reins especially firmly. Even when this is being done the fingers of the left hand should not leave their position between the reins.

The schooling position

The left hand remains in the basic position as before. The right hand has been placed over the right rein in the standard position. With the right hand remaining vertical, the driver grasps the right rein with the bottom three fingers (middle finger, ring finger and little finger) and pulls a short length of rein sideways and to the right without pulling it out of the left hand completely. The length of this 'bridging piece' depends on the size of the driver's hands (it must be long enough for him to be able to turn his hand comfortably inwards and outwards), and also on the horse's level of training. To change from the schooling position back to the standard position, the right hand lifts the rein slightly and places it back in its original position in the left hand. At the same time the index finger of the right hand resumes its position on top of the left rein in order to keep the horses straight. The driver must be able to change from the schooling position to the standard and basic position and back again quickly and without altering the direction of travel or the tempo, and without looking at his hands.

Changing from one position to another should be practised constantly on the driving apparatus. All inadvertent changes in the length of the reins, which if made from the box seat would cause a change of direction, will show up straight away on the driving apparatus.

The schooling position is used for training the horses, to straighten them, in difficult terrain or in dressage tests, unless another position is specifically required (e.g. reins in one hand). The position of the whip (pointing forwards/upwards and to the left) is the same in the schooling position as in the other positions.

The standard position is adopted prior to adjusting the length of one or both reins, when asking for a halt or half-halt, or simply for driving straight ahead. The basic position is used when the right hand is being used to do something else, and to check that the length of the reins is correct.

Taking up the reins (singles and pairs), mounting and getting down

To maintain control when mounting, which is a potentially dangerous time, and when sitting down, and in order to be able to move off promptly if required, even with impatient horses, it is essential to have the reins at the correct length and in the basic position in the hand.

The reins are taken up as follows:

- The driver stands on the left of the horses, level with and facing the saddle or pad, and about a stride away, so that he can reach the horses comfortably with his right arm outstretched.

- With his right hand he takes both reins from under the pad strap or backband and arranges the hand pieces over his forearm from the inside outwards. This prevents the ends of the reins being dropped on the ground and getting dirty.

- The right hand takes hold of the right rein, grain side uppermost, just behind the coupling buckle (with single turnout, just behind the splice). The rein should pass between the index and middle fingers and run down through the hand. The hand establishes a light contact with the horses' mouths. The driver then checks that the reins are not caught on anything. Without losing the contact, the right hand slides down the right rein until the arm is hanging down the right side. The rein is then the correct length and must remain so at all costs.

- The left hand then takes the left rein and places it between the thumb and index finger of the right hand. The driver then adjusts the reins, pushing the left coupling buckle forward until it is 5cm in front of the right one. Since the driver sits on the right-hand side of the vehicle, the left rein has further to travel and needs to be longer by this amount. However, this measurement applies only to pairs of normal-sized horses. With singles and certain types of vehicle the driver may be seated directly

Taking up the reins

behind the horse or horses, or in the centre of the seat, in which case the left rein is not lengthened.

- Both reins are then placed in the basic position in the left hand (index and middle fingers between the reins). To prevent the horses stepping sideways, if there is no groom standing in front the driver should make a big loop in the left rein after he has adjusted the reins to the correct length. The left thumb is placed on top of the loop so that it can be let out gradually as it becomes taut. Otherwise, since the left rein has been lengthened slightly to allow for the driver sitting on the right hand side of the vehicle, there is a risk that if the horses move off prematurely they will turn to the right because the right rein is shorter.

- To mount, the driver walks back to the left front wheel of the vehicle, without taking his eyes off the horses, and climbs up via the step,* holding on to the vehicle with both hands. [*The practice of using the wheel hub as a step when climbing up and down has now been banned because it is dangerous. Some vehicles may need to be modified accordingly.]

- Once on the vehicle, he crosses over to the right-hand side and, as he does so, gradually lets out the loop while maintaining a contact on the horses' mouths. He takes the whip out of the socket and transfers it to the left hand. He then uses his right hand to put the free end of the reins down by his left thigh.

- To get down from the vehicle the driver does the same thing but in reverse. He places the whip in the socket, uses his right hand to place the ends of the reins over his left forearm, stands up and then climbs down backwards from the vehicle without taking his eye off the horses. Once on the ground he places the reins one on top of the other

and pushes them from behind under the pad strap
(or back band with a single).

Shortening and lengthening the reins, turning and reining back

Shortening and lengthening the reins is always performed by the right hand with the reins in the standard position. Letting the reins slip through the
fingers is a very serious fault.

The holds used must be practised in detail on the
driving apparatus. The driver must be able to
shorten and lengthen the reins, both individually
and together, with complete confidence, without
looking down at them and with his attention still
focused on the horses. The better he masters the
handling of the reins with singles and pairs, the easier he will find it with teams and multiples.

Ready to move off

SHORTENING BOTH REINS

There are four different ways of shortening the reins:

- Shortening the reins by a few centimetres. With the reins held in the standard position, the right hand moves forward a few centimetres along both reins and grips
  them. The left hand moves up behind the right, and the driver performs a 'checking'
  action (half-halt) with both hands, and then returns them to their original position.
  The right hand must not be placed too far forward, otherwise the section of rein
  between the hands may fold or twist, or the reins may come out of the left hand.

- By a set amount, moving first one hand then the other down the reins, e.g. prior to a
  right turn. From the standard position, the left hand is placed immediately in front of
  the right, then the right hand further forward still in front of the left, and so into the
  standard position again. Both hands perform a gradual restraining action. This is the
  only exercise in which the left hand is taken off the reins, and is only possible with
  singles and pairs.

- Temporary shortening of the reins, e.g. to perform a half-halt (prior to a halt, a
  change of pace, or lengthening or shortening the stride). With the hands in the standard position, the right hand moves as far as necessary down the reins and checks the
  horses. The left hand moves upwards to make room. After the half-halt has been
  completed, both hands return to their original position. The brake is sometimes used
  at the same time.

• Shortening the reins by a lot, e.g when going downhill or preparing to rein back. The right hand takes hold of both reins behind and below the left hand with the index and middle fingers. The left hand then moves well forward along both reins and closes on them. The right hand returns to the standard position and both hands perform the restraining or 'checking' action. This is the quickest way to shorten the reins, and the most commonly used (especially with teams).

LENGTHENING BOTH REINS

There is only one way to lengthen the reins. The left hand stays put in the basic position. The right hand, in the standard position, slowly draws both reins forward by the same amount through the left hand in the direction of the horses' mouths, and while maintaining a contact with them. When the required length is reached, the right hand returns to the standard position.

• **Lengthening and shortening individual reins**

Lengthening and shortening individual reins requires dexterity, which can only be achieved by constant practice. The whip must remain steady in its correct forward/upward position throughout, and the thong must not disturb the horses.

• **Lengthening the right rein**

With the hands in the standard position, the index finger of the right hand grips the left rein a little more firmly, and acts as a pivot. The right hand makes a twisting movement during which the back of the hand turns to face upwards and the lower three fingers pull the right rein out through the left hand. This movement may be repeated several times if necessary.

• **Shortening the right rein**

To shorten the right rein the procedure is the opposite to that used for lengthening it, i.e. the hand is turned in a clockwise direction, pushing the rein through the slightly open left hand. In this exercise, particular care must be taken not to disturb the horses with the thong of the whip.

• **Lengthening the left rein**

The right hand is in the standard position, with the lower three fingers holding the right rein still. The hand turns clockwise around the little finger, which acts as a pivot, and the right index finger pulls the left rein out through the left hand by a few centimetres. The movement is repeated as often as necessary.

• **Shortening the left rein.**

Here the right hand makes the opposite movement to that used for lengthening the rein, i.e. it turns anti-clockwise and pushes the left rein back through the left hand. It is very difficult to keep the whip still during these exercises, which is why a stick should always be carried as a substitute for a whip when practising on the driving apparatus.

Turns

BASIC OBSERVATIONS

- All turns are made by giving with the outside rein and never by pulling with the inside one. This enables the outside horse to move forward freely and pull the vehicle forwards and round into the turn. For this to work correctly the vehicle must have a fixed splinter bar (with or without swingle trees). (See 'Different types of attachment' p.40.)

- The horses must always be flexed in the direction of the movement, i.e. their heads must not be turned outwards, as happens when they are accustomed to turning at a certain point and do so of their own accord, throwing themselves into the turn without waiting for the driver's rein aids. The correct flexion is obtained by use of the inside rein.

- The driver sits on the right-hand side of the vehicle so that he can use the brake, and to leave space for a passenger. Consequently he is not sitting over the pivot point in the middle of the front axle, but to the right of it, which explains the difference in the rein holds used for the right and left turns.

- When driving on the right-hand side of the road, right turns on busy roads are usually performed at a walk, but left turns may be driven at a collected trot because they follow a wider arc. The driver prepares the horses before each turn by performing a half-halt.

THE LEFT TURN (CORNER)

The driver 'feels' the reins to get the horses' attention. Traffic permitting, the turn may be performed in trot. When driving on the roads, and also in competitions, the driver looks around to check that it is safe to turn and cross the road. The groom or passenger gives the signal with the signalling disc. The driver then looks around again as he begins the turn.

To turn, the driver places his hands in the schooling position. The backs of the hands are turned upwards: first the right hand (this causes the right rein to yield and starts the horses turning), then the left one (which indicates the direction and gives the horses the requisite flexion), with the rein running over the back of the hand. During the turn, both hands move forwards towards the horses to allow them to move through the wide arc required in the left turn. Only in the case of large vehicles or heavy draught is it sometimes necessary for the driver to lengthen the reins slightly before a left turn. To drive straight ahead again, the left hand returns to the upright position (causing the left rein to yield), as does the right hand, so that the hands are once again in the schooling position. The stride can be increased again by giving with both reins again about half way through the turn. If the left (inside) horse comes out of draught during the left turn (which can be seen from the traces), this means that the driver has not yielded the outside rein or has pulled it backwards. If the reins have been lengthened prior to a left hand turn, they must be shortened again after the turn has been completed. Since in Germany the traffic drives on the right, left turns are large radius turns.

LEFT 'U' TURN (ABOUT-TURN TO THE LEFT)

This is used for performing 180° turns on narrow roads *(in countries where the traffic drives on the right)*. First the horses are brought back to a walk. The groom gives the necessary signal as for turning left and, most important, looks around to ensure that the road is clear.

Just before the turn the horses are brought back almost to a halt. Then the turn is started by lengthening the right (outside) rein twice. The right hand must keep a constant contact with the horses' mouths to prevent them from rushing the turn and so also to prevent injury to the coronet from the opposite foot ('treads'). The left hand turns so that the back is uppermost, with the rein running across the back of the hand and not just across the knuckles. Moving the top of the hand towards the right hip in this way has the effect of shortening the left rein. To proceed straight ahead again, the left hand resumes its upright position. Once the turn has been completed, the right hand takes the right rein out of the left hand and takes up a contact until the horses are going straight ahead again on the right-hand side of the road. Then the right rein is placed back in the left hand. If the reins have to be lengthened during the turn, this is achieved by going forward towards the horses' mouths and in the direction of the bend. The reins are held in the basic position for this.

RIGHT TURN (CORNER)

The right turn on the roads is often a tight turn, in which case it is driven at a walk. The appropriate traffic signal should be given about 15m before the turn, and 3m before the turn the horses should be brought back to the required gait and the reins should be placed in the correct position in the hands. If the bend is to be performed in walk, both reins should be shortened slightly. Then the right hand, still holding the whip, takes hold of the right rein about 10–15cm (depending on the individual) in front of the left hand, but does not move it to start with. When the horses reach the point where the wheels of the carriage should start to diverge from the original track, the driver begins the turn by turning his left hand forwards and over (so that the back faces downwards), yielding the left rein. The right hand turns around the whip so as not to disturb its position (it should continue to point forwards/upwards). When the horses' heads and necks are pointing in the new direction, the hands gradually return to their original position, and the reins are lengthened by the same amount that they were previously shortened. On wide modern roads with wide-radius turns, and in dressage arenas, right turns can be performed at a collected trot, without shortening the reins and with the hands in the schooling position.

RIGHT 'U' TURN (ABOUT TURN TO THE RIGHT)

Right 'U' turns are forbidden on roads in Germany, where the traffic drives on the right, and should be avoided also because they are bad for the horses' legs. Since this turn is sometimes required in competitions, it should be learned, but it is not tested in examinations.

TURNS WITH THE REINS IN THE BASIC POSITION

Although the left hand is used on its own only when the right hand is occupied with the brake, whip, etc., a skilful driver should be in a position to shorten and lengthen the stride and change direction using the basic position, i.e. with one hand only. A slightly more positive contact is required with the horses' mouths for this.

CROSSING OVER OR PULLING OUT TO THE LEFT WITH THE REINS IN ONE HAND (E.G. OVERTAKING)

The back of the hand turns backwards and upwards (clockwise) so that the left rein runs across the back of the hand behind the knuckles. At the same time the left hand passes underneath the right hand in the direction of the right hip. To drive straight ahead again the left hand turns back into the upright position and slowly returns to its place in front of the centre of the body.

CROSSING OVER OR PULLING OUT TO THE RIGHT WITH THE REINS IN ONE HAND

The knuckles of the left hand are turned forwards and downwards (anticlockwise) and, with the thumb pointing towards the left thigh, the hand moves left as far as is necessary to perform the turn. For increased effect the thumb and index finger can be pressed on the right rein. To go straight ahead again the left hand turns back to the upright position and slowly returns to its place in front of the centre of the body. In traffic, as with turns performed using the standard and schooling position, the appropriate signal must always be given beforehand with the signalling disc. When using the basic position it is important that the lower three fingers are closed firmly on the reins. Slipping reins can have a disastrous effect on turns and changes of direction and seriously disrupt the orderly way of going of the horses. The rein handling with single turnout is the same as for pairs, only the hand makes smaller movements. With two-wheeled vehicles such as dog carts, it is not necessary to lengthen the reins for a left turn because the distance between the driver's seat and the horse's mouth remains the same.

The rein-back

The rein-back can be performed with the reins held in any of the three positions. First, both reins should be shortened (the amount depends on the horses' level of training). The horses must be securely 'on the aids'. The driver feels the reins (gives an 'asking' rein aid') to get the horses to begin stepping backwards. Once the movement has been 'triggered', the driver must yield the reins sufficiently to allow the horses to balance themselves and then rein back calmly, step by step. These aids may have to be repeated several times. The rein-back is terminated by yielding the reins and lengthening them by the amount they were shortened at the beginning. If the horses rush backwards, this means that the aids were too strong. With young horses it is a good idea to practise the rein back on a slight down slope so that the vehicle can be pushed back more easily. When practising in traffic the use of the voice, namely the command 'Back!' or 'Whoa back!' can be a useful back-up.

AUXILIARY AIDS

THE DRIVING WHIP AND ITS USE

Either a bow-top whip or a drop-thong whip is used depending on the type and style of the turnout. The bow-top whip goes with full-collar harness. The drop-thong whip is used with breastcollar harness. Bow-top whips should be made out of hard, inflexible thornwood. The drop-thong whip, on the other hand, consists of a straight, firm but flexible stick to the end of which a thong is attached. The length of the stick should be such that the thong and lash can be applied, at any time, just behind the pad.

Driving horses must be accustomed to the whip right from the first day of their training. They must understand that the whip is to be respected but not feared. The whip should be in the driver's hand all the time that he is driving. It is an extension of his arm, and his only means of giving effective forward-driving and positioning aids. The whip aids must be given in such a way that they do not disturb the horses in their mouths.

No whip aids can be given effectively unless the horses are wearing blinkers. Since with pairs and multiples there are always differences in temperament, without blinkers the lazy horse or horses would only respond when the whip was raised, whereas the livelier or more reactive horse or horses would be in a state of constant excitement, with their attention focused constantly on the whip.

There are three different kinds of whip aids:

- forward-driving
- collecting, and
- positioning

With the **forward-driving** aids, the driver applies the thong and lash of the whip from the outside, just behind the pad of the horse which is to be sent forward, and yields the rein proportionately, without losing the contact with the horses' mouths.

Applying the whip

In the **collecting aids** the driver maintains a more positive contact with the horses' mouths while at the same time applying the whip behind the pad. The contact must be lightened again afterwards.

With the **positioning aids** the whip is used, behind the pad, to obtain flexion and bend.

When putting the horses to and taking them out, the whip is placed in the socket. If the whip is to keep its shape it must be hung up correctly. The thong should be cleaned and possibly greased after use.

> **Note**: The whip must be long enough for the driver to remain in an upright position when using it.

THE VOICE AND ITS USE

The human voice is an effective medium for influencing the horse's mind. The horse does not understand language, but with its sensitive hearing it can distinguish between different pitches and tones, and between sounds of different duration.

Different sounds have different effects on the horse, e.g.:

- high-pitched short, sharp sounds have the effect of making the horses go forward, and

- low-pitched, soft, drawn-out sounds have a calming and therefore slowing effect.

A person who is in the habit of talking to his horses during his daily dealings with them will be able to use his voice effectively in conjunction with his other aids when driving.

The voice has the same effect on **all** the horses in the pair or team.

Use of the voice in dressage competitions should be avoided.

THE BRAKE AND ITS USE

The foot brake, which has become popular on modern driving vehicles, enables the driver to have both hands on the reins and at the same time to stop the vehicle, and so save the horses from having to do so.

Stopping the vehicle by using the neck as a balancing pole greatly disturbs the horses' balance in transitions, and often causes them to lose rhythm, splay their legs or go sideways. Skilful co-ordination of rein and brake aids in the halts results in horses which are free from resistance, move in rhythm and balance, and readily accept the aids and 'let them through'. *[Durchlässigkeit – literally 'permeability': see 'The Principles of Riding' – Translator.]*

'FEEL' AND REASONING POWERS

The most important qualities in a driver are 'feel' and reasoning powers (the ability to think things through).

The driver needs feel in order to be able to:

- influence the horses (apply the aids) in the correct way,

- influence them (apply the aids) at the right moment,

- apply the aids in the correct intensity, and

- co-ordinate and combine the rein, whip and voice aids in the right proportions.

Reasoning powers are required in order to:

- see what is happening,

- consider what solutions are possible,

- decide how things should be done, and

- put the plan into action, using the appropriate aids.

In the training of the driver, learning and improving 'feel' is an essential prerequisite for refining the use of the aids.

The horse's reaction shows if the aids have been given correctly. This enables the driver to check the correctness and effectiveness of his aids. He learns to distinguish right from wrong, and to put matters right.

Feel is important both in the training of young horses and when working with ready-trained horses. The driver:

- spots the first signs of trouble and can take early preventive or corrective action before faults become established;

- returns without delay to an easier exercise rather than allow resistances to develop;

- promptly identifies the moment when the horse yields or resists and reacts accordingly;

- can tell the difference between high spirits and disobedience;

- can tell whether the horse is simply tired, or whether too much has been asked of it.

> **Note**: Even more important than 'feel' is the ability to think things through, coupled with good powers of observation and the ability to look ahead.

The driver influences the horse through the aids. The following aids are used:

- reins
- whip
- voice
- brake

Used individually the aids cannot be successful; only when they are combined and carefully co-ordinated is it possible to influence the horse in a reliable manner.

The driver must be in a position to use the aids, correctly co-ordinated and in the right intensity, at any point and independently of the horse's movements. The effectiveness of the aids depends on the skill, co-ordination and finesse with which they are used, and not on how strongly they are applied.

The co-ordinated use of the forward-driving and restraining aids has considerable influence on the horse's way of going. These aids should be applied exactly in time with the movement in order to have a correct and lasting effect.

> **Note**: When the forward-driving aids are used in conjunction with the restraining aids, the forward-driving aids must always predominate.

PLAN FOR THE BASIC TRAINING OF THE DRIVER

Driving training must be systematic and progressive. In the following plan the training has been divided up into instruction units, which can be amalgamated or swapped round depending on the facilities available and the student's needs. Each of the individual topics which make up a training unit should be discussed or practised for at least forty-five minutes, but not more than ninety minutes without a break. In addition to the items listed in the following plan, the instructor should not neglect instruction in general horse knowledge.

In Germany, basic training in driving leads to the award of the *Deutsches Fahrabzeichen Klasse IV* (the 'Driving Badge Class 4') in accordance with the Training and Examinations Schedule, the *Ausbildungs- und Prüfungs-Ordnung* or *APO*. At this level the driver should possess practical knowledge and skills in pleasure and sport driving, and be capable of driving unsupervised on a public road.

For this level, approximately 80-120 instruction units are required. The training can take the form of:

- block courses,

- afternoon or evening classes, or

- weekend courses.

DAY 1

Introductory talk about the principles of driving and the aids. On the driving apparatus: basic position, standard position, lengthening and shortening both reins together using the standard position. Harness instruction: harnessing and unharnessing.

DAY 2

Revision exercises. Halts and half-halts. Explanation of differences between right and left turns. Harness instruction: harnessing and unharnessing. Driving practice in the driving training area: moving off, halting, simple turns.

DAY 3

Revision exercises. Harnessing and unharnessing – harness instruction. On the driving apparatus: schooling position (dressage position). Intensive practice in handling the reins: standard position. Schooling position (dressage position). Driving practice in the driving training area. Long-reining.

DAY 4

Revision exercises. Lengthening and shortening individual reins. Practice in turning the hand from the wrist. harnessing up, putting to and taking out, unharnessing. Understanding carriages. Driving practice. Taking up the reins.

DAY 5

Harnessing up, putting to and taking out, unharnessing. On the driving apparatus: turns. Whip aids using the dummy horse. Driving practice: driver exercises and dressage tests in the driven dressage arena, the driving training area and in traffic.

DAY 6

Instruction in the different types of coupling reins and the theory of coupling rein adjustment. Driving practice as above.

DAY 7

Revision exercises. Explanation of the different parts of the harness. Different kinds of turnout. Driving practice as above.

DAY 8

Revision exercises. Driving practice across country.

DAY 9

Revision exercises. Driving practice. Talk on training young horses to harness.

DAY 10

Revision exercises. Driving practice.

DAY 11

Revision exercises.

> **Note**: Special emphasis should be placed from the outset on the actual driving practice.

3

Basic Training of the Horse

Aims and requirements

When training a horse to harness, the aim is to produce an animal which is steady even in heavy traffic but at the same time forward-going and a pleasure to drive. As a rule, the primary use of today's driving horse is no longer as a draught animal in agriculture or commerce. It is now used mainly in the leisure industry, either for recreation and relaxation or in sport. In order to meet the requirements of this new role, not only will the horse itself need to fulfil certain criteria, but it will also need a trainer who is skilled in this field. Newcomers to the sport tend to think that driving horses, and particularly ponies, is 'child's play'. This is quite wrong and can be highly dangerous.

A good driver and trainer who has taken the trouble to get to know and understand young horses will appreciate that the result of correct basic training is a horse which is happy and free-moving. In driving and driving training, the importance of the horse's **inner well-being** cannot be overemphasised, and is the most important criterion for judging the harmony between driver and horse.

Behaviour and early training

Horses usually mature at the age of four or five. At the age of three or three and a half, after a few weeks' familiarisation with the harness, the vehicle, roads and traffic, the young horse can be turned away for a few months to finish growing and mature. Training can then start again at the age of three and a half to four years.

To ensure that the horse is not overstretched both physically and mentally, the trainer needs experience not only of driving but also of animal psychology. Horses are easily upset and spoiled by incorrect treatment. It takes months, or often years, to over-come problems which arise in this way. Other consequences are injuries, especially to the limbs, and a shortened working life.

The following **psychological guidelines** may be of use in handling and training the horse:

- Physically and by nature the horse is a highly specialised creature of flight; it is also a herd animal, and feels safest when it is amongst others of its kind.

- The horse sees man as one of its kind; as the horse's teacher, man needs to take the place of a horse higher in the hierarchy or 'pecking order'.

- This is achieved through understanding and not by force – when the horse makes the wrong response to man's instructions, this is because it has not understood cor-rectly.

- To be able to understand the trainer, the horse needs to **trust** him – understanding is based on trust.

- Man communicates with the horse through the aids and the auxiliary aids, i.e. the voice, touch and reward.

- The horse will only understand the trainer's instructions properly if it has been familiarised with the aids. The horse's primitive, instinctive reaction is to run away from strange or unfamiliar objects and situations, and it needs to be acquainted with them slowly and systematically. If fear or uncertainty arise, the trainer must start again from the beginning. He must also bear in mind that the horse has an excellent **memory** – it remembers both the good and the bad things which happen to it, and it can take a long time to forget a bad experience.

- For the horse to be able to learn, it must be sufficiently mature physically. Making excessive physical or mental demands will cause setbacks in the horse's training.

- The horse will achieve its full potential only if its needs are met and it is in harmony with its environment – of which man is a part.

- The horse must associate man with **security** in every situation.

The trainer must also understand the role of the horse's **senses.** Of these, **smell** is the most highly developed, although it is rarely possible to put it to good use in the train-ing. It does, however, exercise a negative influence at times, for example when the horse resists because of a smell it dislikes (e.g. a pig-farm or field of pigs), or which brings back unpleasant memories (smoke or the smell of chemicals or drugs).

The horse's **hearing** is also highly developed. It is for this reason that any unneces-sary loud noises should be avoided in the stable and during training.

The horse's **sight** is not very well developed. However, owing to the position of the eyes on the side of the head, the horse has a much wider field of vision than man, i.e. than the driver.

The horse has an exceptional ability to see movement. It sees moving things in particular (including to the sides and in the distance) more clearly and sooner than does its driver, so that the driver often has no idea why the horse has shied.

The horse's sense of **touch** and its **sensitivity to touch** are very highly developed. It is this sensitivity which allows the trainer to fine-tune the 'touch' aids (in driving, the whip aids).

Observing the horse's eyes, ears, tail and breathing, and watching the skin for signs of sweating can give the trainer vital information on the horse's mental state.

The **eyes** reflect the horse's state of mind. They can express attentiveness, confidence, mistrust or fear. The **ear movements** can also provide vital information about the horse's emotional state. Laid-back or flattened ears always indicate that the horse is ill at ease and ready to defend itself or resist. Mobile or pricked ears denote attentiveness and a willing attitude.

Snorting or 'sneezing', in conjunction with a freely carried, swinging tail indicate that the horse is free from tension and working, or ready to work. A tail which is tensed, clamped down or carried abnormally high is a sign of fear, tension or excitement.

Sweating can be caused by excitement as well as by exertion. It is usually accompanied by raised heart and respiration rates.

The most important qualities required in a trainer are understanding, sensitivity, calmness, consistency and a logical mind. Nervous, highly strung people are usually impatient, and do not have the necessary calm, objective approach. Constant repetition of practices necessary for safe handling of the horse, such as tying it up, lifting up the feet, leading, and making it stand, will help to establish a habit of obedience in the horse. Rewarding, chastising, and the appropriate punishment, where necessary, must always be related directly to what has happened or what it is hoped to achieve. Constantly feeding the horse sugar, carrots and other titbits for no particular reason will spoil it and eventually lead to a reversal of the man-horse 'pecking order'. Unreasonable or disproportionate punishment, on the other hand, will lead to resistance, and may eventually make the horse vicious and dangerous.

In training horses it is a big mistake to expect the horse's reactions to be based on thought processes similar to those of man. Horses, like all animals, will always act in response to primitive, inborn reflexes. Only if the trainer familiarises himself with the basic principles of horse psychology will he succeed in his task. Good conformation, combined with good paces, a good temperament and systematic schooling, or 'gymnasticising', are the best foundations for the development of balance and self-carriage. It is the trainer's responsibility to use his skill, combined with patience and constant observation, to get the horse to co-operate willingly. The musculature needs to be developed gradually so as to enable the horse to regain its natural balance, and then later to enable more of the weight to be transferred onto the hindquarters.

THE BASIC GAITS

One of the aims of schooling is to preserve and refine the purity and regularity of the natural gaits of the horse when it is being driven. It is therefore essential that the trainer understands exactly how the horse moves in each of the three basic gaits, because only then will he be in a position to take the appropriate action to refine and improve them.

> **Note**: The rhythm must be maintained in each of the basic gaits, and in each form of the trot, i.e. working, collected and extended.

WALK

The walk is a marching movement, in four-time, without a moment of suspension, and with the feet set down one after another in a series of **steps**. The forward movement of the feet can be broken down into eight phases, with the horse being supported alternately by three, then two legs. Hence the feet are moved forward in an alternating diagonal-lateral sequence – for example: right fore, left hind, left fore, right hind. The easiest way to check that the footfalls are in regular four-time is to listen to the hoof beats on a hard surface. The 'beat' can then be heard clearly. It is also helpful to watch the foreleg and hind leg on the same side: seen from the ground they should on no account be parallel or nearly parallel. In fact they should form a 'V' shape for a brief moment, with the hind foot, as it swings forward, almost touching the forefoot. If the feet on the same side are moved forward and set down simultaneously, the horse is performing an incorrect gait known as 'pacing'.

> **Note**: In driving, in walk the horse is required to be 'on the bit'. It should be regular, and should 'flow' and cover the ground.

TROT

The trot is a two-time movement consisting of four phases. The legs are picked up, carried forward and set down in diagonal pairs. Since one diagonal pair is picked up

Walk

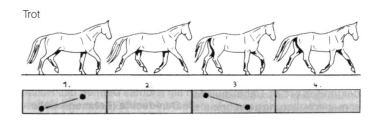

Trot

Right canter

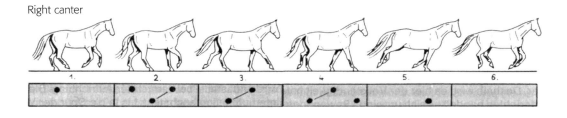

Left canter

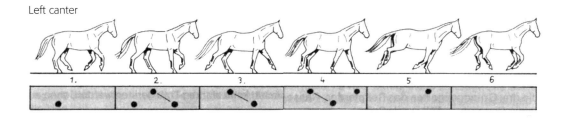

Rein back

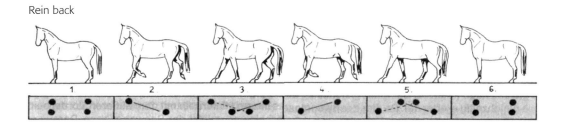

before the other is set down, there is a moment of suspension in between. The following forms of trot are recognised.

The **working trot** is the form most frequently used in basic training, both under saddle and in harness, and particular attention should therefore be paid to it. The horse should work with 'looseness' (German: *Losgelassenheit*) and should take regular, ground-covering steps full of impulsion, i.e. it should work energetically from behind. The hind feet should be set down approximately in the prints of the forefeet.

The horse is then encouraged to go forward more energetically and **lengthen its strides**. It covers more ground without quickening its steps. The powerful thrust of the hind feet enables the forefeet to be raised and carried lightly and freely. The hind feet are set down in front of the prints of the forefeet.

The neck is lengthened slightly, bringing the nose a little further in front of the vertical, i.e. the frame is lengthened. The horse should continue to yield through its poll, and should remain in self-carriage.

As the impulsion and thrust of the hindquarters develops, the horse can be asked to perform the even more ground-covering and expressive **extended trot**, which is the ultimate expression of forward movement in trot. The horse should show as much impulsion and forward thrust as possible, and cover as much ground as possible, and at the same time should lengthen its frame proportionately. This is achieved by stretching the neck and bringing the nose forward. The hind feet should be set down well in front of the prints of the forefeet.

It is important that the horse does not rush, and that the rhythm is maintained. Only if the horse can be collected, and so take more of its weight onto its hindquarters, will it be able to perform extended trot without falling onto its forehand.

In the **collected trot** there is increased flexion of the hindquarter joints (haunches), and the hind legs engage further under the horse's body in the direction of the centre of gravity. Hence the steps cover less ground, but the energy, activity and impulsion are maintained. There is less weight on the forehand, and the horse is higher in front and shorter in its body, i.e. it is more 'upright'. The steps are also higher. The hind feet are set down no further forward than the prints of the forefeet. Extended and collected trot are difficult to obtain when pulling heavy weights.

> **Note**: In driving, the trot is judged by its rhythm, impulsion and ground-covering capacity.

CANTER

The canter is a three-time gait consisting of a series of jump-like movements, in between which there is a moment of suspension. The canter may be 'on the left leg' (left canter) or 'on the right leg' (right canter), depending on which pair of legs steps further forward. The sequence is as follows: first the outside hind leg, then the inside hind leg and the outside foreleg together, followed by the inside foreleg, and finally the moment of suspension. Hence the left canter, for example, is made up of the following phases:

- right hind foot on the ground (one-point base of support),

- right hind, left hind and right fore on the ground together (three-point base of support),

- left hind and right fore (diagonal pair) on the ground (two-point base of support),

- left hind and right fore, plus left fore (three-point base of support again),

- left fore only on the ground (one-point base of support again),

- moment of suspension.

> **Note**: Canter is not compulsory in driving. However, it may be used:
>
> - between the start and the finish in obstacle driving;
>
> - inside the penalty zone of the marathon obstacles;
>
> - during the awards ceremony (teams only);
>
> - in exceptional cases during the marathon, such as in heavy going or on steep slopes.

REIN-BACK

Although not one of the basic paces, the rein-back also has a designated sequence, and so is included here to complete the picture. The rein-back is a two-time stepping movement in which the feet are picked up, moved back and set down in diagonal pairs. One diagonal pair of feet is set down before the other is picked up, so there is no moment of suspension (suspension phase).

TRAINING

A turnout is judged by the way of going and performance of the horse, or of each of the horses. Skilful early training of each individual horse is therefore essential. The horse's reliability in harness depends on knowledgeable, quiet, patient early handling and training to harness. Mistakes made at this stage are usually impossible to put right.

The training method and the precautions to be taken depend on the horse's temperament. Quiet, knowledgeable handling is the first requirement for successful training. Excitement, shouting and running should be avoided in the training environment. Force should not be used, even with a horse which is excitable or difficult to start with.

Any horse can be trained with patience, provided the trainer knows how to assess and overcome any problems which arise. A horse cannot be forced to pull!

Training potential harness horses under saddle to start with is a good idea. A horse which is used to carrying a saddle, and accustomed to the weight of the rider, will take more kindly and readily to being driven. As with a riding horse, the aims in training the driving horse are as follows:

HANDLING IN THE STABLE

In most cases the horse's basic training takes place in a different environment from that in which it grew up. Getting it used to its **new surroundings**, **stable and diet** is the first priority, and an essential prerequisite for the horse's future development and training. The trainer must be prepared to use tact and patience, and take the necessary time over this. Usually a few days will suffice, but in some cases several weeks may be required.

During the period when the horse is first being put to and driven, turning it out more in the field or exercise area will help to work off excessive energy, relieve tension, and keep it happy and well adjusted.

Particular care should be taken when familiarising the horse with the **harness**. It is best to introduce this in the familiar surroundings of the horse's stable. The pleasant associations of the stable (food!) will help it to accept the unfamiliar equipment.

First the bridle is put on. It is a good idea to attach a lunge line to the bridle to enable the trainer to keep control if the horse pulls away unexpectedly. If it manages to break free of the harness when it is put on for the first time, it can take a long time to get it to accept it calmly.

To start with, many horses dislike the girth being tightened, and the pad should be put on for the first time in the school, or at least in a yard where there is plenty of room.

Even if the horse is used to the handlers, and has been familiarised beforehand with the harness, it will still often give a few more or less lively bucks to try to get rid of it. This could lead to serious injury if it is in the stable, or even worse in the stable corridor at the time.

The trainer should always work with an assistant, never alone. A quiet manner and a reassuring voice are important. Food can be used as a reward during training.

LUNGEING

Lungeing is a very effective, and in many cases essential preparatory stage in the horse's training. The aim of lungeing is:

- to get the horse used to the harness and the work,

- to teach it obedience, and

• to develop rhythm and looseness (*Losgelassenheit*).

Lungeing is also useful in later training for correcting faults in the horse's gaits and position. It is beneficial for correcting the horse as a whole, and also for improving problem areas such as the neck and back. Another use is for giving light exercise to a horse which has been ill, or simply to provide variety in the training.

When teaching the horse to lunge, the trainer should be accompanied by an assistant. The lunger stands in the centre while the assistant leads the horse out onto the circle, then walks round next to its head. Once the lunger and the helper feel that the horse will stay on the circle of its own accord, the assistant can walk back to the centre, take the whip, and then position himself level with the horse's hind legs and follow it round on the circle.

It is important that this work is carried out in a calm environment and that the trainer is clear and consistent in his instructions. The horse will then learn very quickly to respond to the lunge, whip and voice aids, and will soon be lungeing freely on both reins.

To begin with the side-reins should either not be fitted or should be fitted loosely, and the horse should therefore be lunged in a special lunge ring or other confined area. As a rule the trainer can start to use side-reins (single side-reins or double 'running reins') after three or four days. They should be attached to the surcingle or girth approximately at shoulder height so that when the horse flexes its neck, its mouth is approximately level with its shoulder joint. The nose should be about 10cm in front of the vertical. It should never be behind the vertical.

The side-reins should be of equal length so as not to interfere with the horse's natural balance, and not to encourage crookedness. When the horse starts to lower its head and seek the contact, it must be allowed to do so. The trainer can use the lunge rein to obtain the necessary flexion to the inside.

The correct length and height of the side-reins is determined through experience and observation. The aim is for the horse to learn to 'go into' them and seek a contact. Particularly in the early stages, the young horse should be lunged for no more than 20–30 minutes. There should be frequent changes of rein, and the horse should be given plenty of praise.

Further guidelines on lungeing young, and older, horses are contained in Book 6 in the German series, *Lungeing*.

WORK ON LONG REINS

Before beginning the work on long reins, the horse must first be taught to lunge (see *The Principles of Riding*, and *Lungeing* in the German series). Long-reining prepares the horse for the rein aids and teaches it what they mean. Also, the outside rein running around the hind legs just above the hocks prepares the horse for the contact of the harness, especially the traces. Ticklish horses which would otherwise kick and endanger the vehicle and the driver can be safely put to once they have been familiarised with long reins. Even apparently quiet, easy-going horses sometimes kick when they are being long-reined. Hence no horse should be put to without first being trained on long reins, and this should be done so thoroughly that the horse will not kick when it is attached to the vehicle. Re-training horses which have been put to prematurely is very time-consuming, and bad habits are extremely difficult to eradicate.

For long-reining, as for lungeing, the horse's forelegs should be bandaged, and brushing boots should be fitted on the hind legs, especially if the horse is shod.

The other equipment is described below.

● The bridle
In the early stages of training, an ordinary riding bridle with a plain, thick, single-jointed snaffle is used, then a driving bridle with a snaffle bit. The horse must be familiarised gradually with the blinkers.

● The harness
The traces should be removed and the trace buckles attached to the point strap on the pad. The pad should be fitted with a crupper. With pairs harness the false belly band should be done up so that it is against the horse and not hanging loosely. The point strap should be adjusted so that the trace buckle lies against the horse's side approximately level with the point of the shoulder. A large ring approximately 10cm in diameter should be attached on either side at the point where the trace buckle is attached to the belly band. The long reins are passed through these rings (one on the inside, one on the outside).

● The long reins
The total length of the two reins should be at least 16–17m. They are attached to the bit rings by means of buckles or spring clips. It is a good idea to have the long reins made up all in one piece, i.e. without a buckle to get in the way. It also makes things easier if the first 2m or so of each rein at the bit end is made of rolled leather to enable them to slide more easily through the rings on the pad or breaking roller. Two lunge reins joined together, or a long pair of single harness reins can be used as a substitute for a pair of long reins, though the join or buckle in the middle will get in the way.

● The lungeing or long-reining whip
A whip of the type used for lungeing is also suitable for long-reining (this is described in *Lungeing*, Book 6 of the German series). For long-reining the trainer should be dressed in such a way that he can move freely. Leather gloves are a good idea. The area used for long-reining should be in a quiet location.

The trainer should stand in the middle of the circle. Ideally he should hold both reins in one hand so as to leave the other hand free to use the whip correctly. However, with a young horse in the early stages of training it will be necessary to hold a rein in

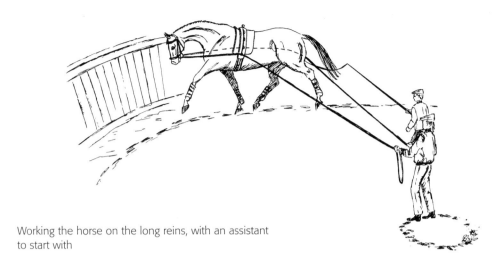

Working the horse on the long reins, with an assistant
to start with

each hand and to have an assistant to handle the whip. Once this stage is past, holding
the reins in the basic position has been found to give good results. When long-reining
to the left, the reins are held in the left hand, with the left rein running over the knuckle
of the index finger, and the outside (right) rein between the second and third fingers of
the left hand. If the ends of the reins are too long, they can be hooked up on the little
finger. The right hand carries the whip, the end of which points towards the horse's
hind legs. As in driving (standard and schooling positions) the right hand may also
assist with the outside (right) rein if necessary.

When long-reining to the right, the whip is held in the left hand. The right hand
holds the reins, so that the outside (left) rein passes between the second and third fingers of the right hand, and the inside (right) rein runs between the thumb and the
index finger down through the palm of the hand. Here again the end of the reins may
be hooked over the little finger, and the left hand can assist with the rein handling as
required.

When first teaching the horse to lunge it is sometimes advisable to run the inside
rein straight back to the hand, as in ordinary lungeing, rather than passing it through
the ring on the pad or the rein terret on the collar. The horse must be familiarised with
the outside rein gradually. Again it is a good idea to run it straight over the back ini-
tially, and then put it around the hindquarters towards the end of the lesson. The horse
will then soon get used to it. If it does kick at first, it should not jabbed in the mouth as
a punishment. Instead, the trainer should simply keep the horse going forward and
ensure that it does not get the outside rein caught between its hind legs. Once the horse
is used to being long-reined, both the outside and the inside reins can be put through
the rings attached to the pad and the hame terrets or neckstrap rings on the collar or
breastcollar respectively.

The trainer walks round in a small circle in the centre. He should face and look into
the direction of the movement. The outside rein, which comes round the back of the

horse's legs, should never be so tight that it restricts the horse's movement. The horse is steered with the inside rein; the outside rein has a regulating effect, like the outside 'guarding' leg in riding (see *The Principles of Riding*). When the horse is in movement the outside rein should remain at all times above the level of the hocks.

With horses which are used to being long-reined, changes of rein are performed in movement. To start with, the changes are performed 'out of the circle', then later 'through the circle', as described (for training under saddle) in *The Principles of Riding* and in *Lungeing*. The change of rein is performed at first in walk, but it can be driven later in a short, balanced trot. Performing the change with the reins held in the schooling position (i.e. as when driving from the vehicle) is a good method. However, changing the whip from one hand to the other requires practice. Later in the training the horse is driven out of the circle and along straight lines in the school, with the trainer positioned behind the horse and between the two reins.

> **Note**: When long-reining, the trainer keeps an equal contact on both reins and is also responsible for carrying the whip.

ACCUSTOMING THE HORSE TO THE HARNESS AND THE EQUIPMENT

Nowadays most horses have been accustomed to people from an early age. Wearing a headcollar and having its feet picked up and handled is not new to the horse. For accustoming a horse to wearing harness it is best to use breastcollar harness at first. It is light, can be adjusted to fit any horse, and fulfils the purpose of getting the young horse used to pressure on its chest when it pulls.

Special care should be taken when introducing the horse to the crupper. With very sensitive horses, fitting the crupper should be delayed until the horse has been worked and is no longer fresh. The first time it is put on there should be an assistant present to divert the horse's attention, hold up one of its forefeet and generally help with the safety precautions. The horse will find it easier to accept the crupper if it is used to having its tail lifted and its dock sponged and wiped as part of its daily grooming routine.

It is not enough simply to put the harness on: it must also be worked while wearing it. At first it is a good idea to lead it in hand with the harness on. However, unnecessary pieces of harness should not be allowed to hang down and hit the horse's legs, which will only irritate and upset it. The more time the trainer spends in the early days getting the horse used to the harness, the easier the later training will be.

It is a good idea to use an ordinary riding bridle in the early stages of training, and to use the driving bridle with blinkers only when the horse is used to the harness and the feel of the long reins around its hind legs.

Familiarising the horse with the harness will only take a few days if the trainer goes about it quietly and patiently.

> **Note**: If the horse is upset and put off at this point in its training, it is usually a difficult and time-consuming task to get it back on track.

TRAINING THE HORSE TO PULL A SLEDGE

Driving the horse to a sledge is one of several ways of preparing it to pull a cart. As with long-reining, a set of single harness or half of a set of pairs harness can be used for this purpose. When the horse has been given a work-out on the lunge or long reins to get rid of any tension, an assistant attaches a rope about 3m long to the end of each trace, while a second assistant holds the horse's head and keeps it occupied.

Once the traces have been lengthened, the trainer takes up the long reins and positions himself behind the horse. Each of the assistants holds one of the traces at a safe distance from the horse's hind legs. To begin with, the assistants should be positioned more to the side of than behind the horse, to prevent the traces touching it.

The trainer then asks the horse to walk on, and the assistants exert a gentle pull on the traces. As the lesson progresses, and the horse learns to accept the pressure on its chest, the pull can be increased. If the horse ceases to go forward, the pressure should be eased at first, so as not to encourage resistance.

When the horse is coping calmly with this work, the traces can be allowed to make contact with the horse's body and hindquarters. Horses which have been properly and skilfully prepared through work on long reins usually accept this without problems. The horse is worked on straight lines to start with, but as soon as possible the exercise should be performed on curved and circular tracks because this also brings the long reins in contact with the horse. Once the horse is coping with this (and the trainer should not forget to praise it regularly), the lesson should be ended for the day.

This work should be repeated over the next few days, then as soon as possible, when the horse will go forward willingly 'into its collar', it can be harnessed to a sledge about two and a half metres long by attaching the ends of the traces to two rings on the front of the sledge. There should be sufficient distance between the horse and the front of the sledge to prevent the horse's feet coming into contact with the sledge if it starts kicking. Also, the traces must be able to be released easily from the sledge in case of emergency.

Once the traces are attached to the sledge, an assistant leads the horse on, while the trainer, holding the long reins, remains behind the horse. At first, the exercise should be performed on a surface where it will not make too much noise. However, the horse must then be gradually familiarised not only with the contact of the traces and the pressure on its chest when it pulls, but also with the noise made by the sledge, and later the carriage.

Here again, the horse should be worked as soon as possible on curved and circular tracks, with the outside trace in contact with the horse's hind leg. An assistant should lead the horse to begin with, but if it stays calm the trainer can then control it solely with the long reins.

When the horse has been performing this exercise calmly for a few days, weights can be placed on the sledge so that the horse is gradually asked to put more weight into its collar in order to pull it. It is essential that the horse accepts the contact of the traces, and at some point one of the traces should be run between its hind legs, because it needs to be able to accept this too without panicking.

Once the horse remains calm and relaxed throughout this work, it can progress to pulling a carriage.

PUTTING TO AND TRAINING THE HORSE TO PULL A CARRIAGE

A solidly built, safe, free-running vehicle is essential for this purpose. On no account must the driver's seat be too low, which would be dangerous, as well as preventing him from observing the horse.

This lesson should take place on soft but not too deep going. A 'breaking cart' is recommended, with the pole (or shafts') attachment point well above the ground to prevent the horse 'kicking over the pole (or shafts)'. The vehicle must have a fixed bar with swingle trees. A fixed bar is the only system which allows the driver to control the distribution of work. The horse should be attached to the carriage for the first time when it has already been given a good work-out in front of the sledge. The schoolmaster should already have been put to, on the right of the pole, and be stood waiting. The young horse should be placed on the left side to start with, since this is safer for the driver if it kicks. As he gets up onto the vehicle, the driver must take care not to touch the croup of the young horse with the reins. When training the horse later on the road, placing the young horse on the right of the pole will help keep it away from on-coming and overtaking traffic (in countries which drive on the right). Regularly changing sides is recommended since it is beneficial to the horse's training.

When putting to for the first time the following method has been shown to give good results. The young horse, wearing a headcollar under its driving bridle, is brought alongside the pole. At this point it may be tied, by a rope attached to its headcollar, to the other horse's pole strap. It is recommended that, for safety reasons, an assistant leads the horse from the outside with a rope. The horse must be able to hold its head straight, i.e. its head should not be pulled towards the other horse. The coupling reins can then be fastened to the bits, and the pole strap done up. Finally the traces are attached in the order already explained: first the outside trace, then the inside one. It is a good idea to have another helper praising the horse and distracting it with food.

The driver must mount very carefully. If the horse stands quietly the driver should not move off straight away, but instead allow the horse to get used to his movements on the seat and on the vehicle. When he moves off it should be slightly to the right, with the assistant still at the young horse's head. By this method the more experienced horse does the pulling and steers the young horse smoothly in the direction of the movement with the pole strap. On no account must the helper on the ground hold the horse tightly with the rope or lunge rein. His job is simply to ensure that the young horse does not turn its head towards its neighbour, rub or bang itself against the pole, or try to run away. The lessons should not be too long at first, and the horses should be taken out of the vehicle in front of the stable so that the young horse remains as calm as possible.

In the early lessons, if the young horse breaks into a trot the driver should not try to stop it. However, as the training progresses he should gradually confirm and establish the walk. Walking also serves to calm the horse and give it confidence. It is better to take the trouble to teach the horse to walk calmly, and so produce a steady, safe driving horse than to rush through this stage and end up with a horse which is unsettled, excitable and unreliable for years to come.

The care of the horse after the training session is of special importance. Every time the harness is taken off, all the areas of the body that come in contact with the harness should be washed down very carefully with cold water. If any sore places are revealed, the horse should not be worked again in harness until the sores have healed completely and are no longer sensitive to the touch. Even with experienced horses, careful attention should be paid to the areas underneath the collar or breastcollar.

Even when the horse is quite happy pulling the vehicle, if the harness is changed, for example from breastcollar to full collar, or the horse is changed over to the other side of the pole, the trainer should proceed with extreme caution.

Dressage training (basic flatwork)

The 'scales of training' (the building blocks)

Training a horse is not simply a matter of 'breaking it in'. It is more a programme of systematic gymnastic training and suppling, aimed at developing to the full the horse's physical and mental aptitudes and turning it into an obedient riding or driving horse with a broadly based training – in fact, a horse which is a pleasure to work with.

The training programme sets out, in the order they are obtained, the basic qualities of the schooled horse, and the phases in the development of these qualities.

The training process consists of three phases, which can be further divided into six

Note: The training of every horse should meet the criteria laid down in the 'Scales of Training', irrespective of the horse's intended use. A horse trained accordingly will respond obediently, harmoniously and without tension to the rider's aids.

sub-sections. None of the six concepts which form the basis of these sub-sections can be considered in isolation – they are all interdependent. They must be developed in accordance with a systematic plan, but not singly or in a rigid order.

The diagram shows how the three main stages of training overlap, and the links between the different concepts.

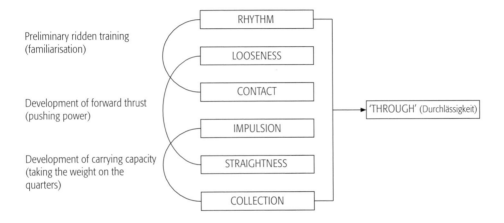

For a driving horse, the qualities set out in the 'Scales of Training' are essential, whether the horse is intended for competition or leisure use. It should have received the same systematic basic training so that is sufficiently supple and 'lets the driver's aids through' at all times. This ensures that it can be driven harmoniously, and also helps to keep it sound.

The 'Scales of Training' are used both:

- for the systematic basic training of the young horse, and

- with an older horse as the basis for the training session (i.e. each individual lesson contains this training plan in a condensed form).

Note: The attainment of these individual training goals depends on the horse undergoing an all-round gymnastic training ('gymnasticising') and on the trainer being mentally attuned to the horse.

Throughout the training, great emphasis should be placed on variety.

A horse which is supple and 'through' (*Durchlässigkeit*) as a result of correct training is more obedient and agile, and is a pleasure to drive. This applies not only to competition horses, but to all horses, whatever they are used for, including generalised sport driving and pleasure driving.

> **Note**: The overall aim of training is a horse which is supple and 'through'. The development of this quality runs parallel to that of the other qualities.

Rhythm

The term 'rhythm' refers to the regularity of the steps or strides in each of the three gaits: they should cover equal distances and also be of equal duration. For example, in working trot the step taken by one diagonal should cover the same amount of ground as the other, and the beat should be regular.

To be able to judge the correctness of the rhythm, the trainer needs to understand exactly how the horse moves in each of the gaits.

> **Note**: The rhythm must be maintained through transitions and turns as well as on straight lines. No exercise or movement can be considered good if it contains rhythm faults, i.e. if the rhythm is lost. Furthermore, the training is incorrect if it results in rhythm faults.

Looseness (Losgelassenheit)

Looseness is a prerequisite for all further training and, along with rhythm, is an essential aim of the preliminary training. Even if the rhythm is maintained, the movement cannot be considered correct unless the horse is swinging and working through its back, and the muscles are contracting and expanding without tension.

Only if the horse is physically and mentally free from tension or constraint (in German *Zwanglosigkeit*) can it work with looseness, use itself to the full and achieve its full potential. The horse's joints should bend and straighten equally on both sides of its body, and the horse should convey the impression that it is putting its whole mind, as well as its body, into its work.

Indications of looseness (and mental relaxation) are:

• a contented, happy expression (eyes, ear movements);

- a rhythmically swinging back;

- a closed but not 'dead' mouth (the horse should mouth the bit gently every so often);

- tail lifted slightly ('carried') and swinging in time with the movement;

- 'snorting', which is a sign that the horse is mentally relaxed.

> **Note**: Looseness has been achieved when the horse will stretch its head and neck forwards and downwards in all three gaits. A horse working with looseness should swing through its back and move with rhythmic, unspoilt natural paces; it should not rush forwards, quickening its steps, i.e. run.

Contact

Contact is the soft, steady, elastic connection between the driver's hand and the horse's mouth. The horse should go forwards, rhythmically and with looseness, from the forward-driving aids and 'seek' a contact with the driver's hand. The horse is then said to go into the contact. The driver, for his part, keeps a steady, soft contact with the horse's mouth: as they say in Germany: 'the horse seeks the contact and the driver provides it'.

This correct, steady contact allows the horse to find its balance in its work in harness, and to find a rhythm in each of the gaits. The poll is always the highest point of the neck, except when the horse is being 'sent forwards and downwards', i.e. driven in an extended outline.

> **Note**: The contact should never be achieved by a backward action of the hands; it should result from the correctly delivered forward thrust of the hind legs. The horse should go confidently forward into the contact in response to the forward-driving aids.

Taking a contact gradually evolves into being 'on the bit', which entails flexion at the poll. This should not be considered as an aim in itself. The horse should come onto the bit as a consequence and by-product of correct schooling. Hence when working with young horses at the basic stage of training, or when performing 'loosening' work with older, more experienced horses, the driver should avoid trying to 'get the horse onto the bit' prematurely. Especially if this is achieved by use of the hands alone, this detracts from the looseness and the activity of the hind legs, and so defeats the whole object of the training.

Impulsion

A horse is said to have impulsion when the energy created by the hind legs is being transmitted into the gait and into every aspect of the forward movement. A horse can be said to be working with impulsion when it pushes off energetically from the ground and swings its feet well forward.

To be able to work with impulsion in trot or canter, the horse needs first to be able to show looseness (*Losgelassenheit*), a springy, swinging back and a soft, correct contact. Impulsion is only possible in the trot and canter. There can be no impulsion in walk because there is no moment of suspension.

The impulsion is good if the hocks are carried energetically forwards and upwards immediately after the feet leave the ground, rather than being carried only upwards, or even being drawn backwards. The movements are absorbed by the horse's back muscles.

> **Note**: Impulsion is the result of correct training. The trainer makes use of the horse's natural paces, but adds to them looseness, forward thrust (originating in the hindquarters) and suppleness (*Durchlässigkeit*).

If the horse is pushed too hard so that it rushes and quickens its steps, the moment of suspension (suspension phase) is shortened because it puts its feet down sooner. Even if the rhythm is maintained, if the tempo is too fast the impulsion will suffer as a result.

Straightness

A horse is said to be straight when its forehand is in line with its hindquarters, that is when the horse's longitudinal axis is in line with the straight or curved track which it is following. In Germany the horse is then said to be 'covering the track'. Straightness is necessary in order for the weight to be evenly distributed over the two halves of the body. It is developed through systematically training and suppling ('gymnasticising') both sides of the body equally.

Most horses are naturally crooked. Like right- and left-handedness in humans, this crookedness has its origins in the brain, and is something the horse is born with. Also, the horse's shoulders are narrower than its hindquarters, which further encourages it to be crooked.

In most cases, the horse's right hind foot is set down further to the right than the right forefoot. As a result, the right hind leg has to push harder, while the left hind leg has to bend more. This also puts more strain on the left foreleg.

If the hind legs are required to deliver more power, and so bend more, the left hind leg will be able to do so, but the right leg will try to avoid the increased flexion by stepping sideways, outside the track of the right forefoot.

Straightness is necessary for the following reasons:

- so that the horse's weight is evenly distributed on both sides, and to avoid excessive wear and tear on the limbs on one side;

- in order to optimise the forward thrust, i.e. to enable the horse to push equally and effectively with its hind legs;

- so that the driver can keep the horse securely on the aids and the horse can 'let the aids through';

- to enable the horse to go equally into the contact on both sides;

- in order to obtain be able to develop collection.

Only if the horse is straight can it be equally supple and 'through' (*Durchlässigkeit*) on both reins.

> **Note**: If the horse is straight, the hind legs will push exactly in the direction of the centre of gravity. The restraining aids will then also pass through the horse correctly, via the mouth, poll, neck and back to the hindquarters, and they will act on both hind legs equally.

Straightening the horse is a never-ending task, since every horse has some degree of natural crookedness, which is exacerbated by driving it with a pole on one side!

Straightness is a precondition for collection, since only if the horse is straight can the weight be transferred onto both hind legs equally.

Collection

The aim of all the gymnastic training is to create a horse which is useful, and ready and willing to work. For the horse to meet these conditions, its weight must be distributed as evenly as possible over all four legs. This means transferring some of the weight from the forehand equally onto each hind leg.

> **Note:** The horse is built in such a way that there is more weight on its forehand than on its hindquarters. Training the horse to take more of its weight on its quarters makes it safer to ride (allowing it to balance and keep its footing) and helps to keep it sound. Every horse will therefore benefit from some degree of collection.

> **Note**: The slow, active, balanced trot commonly used in driving should not be confused with a collected trot. When driving slowly, the steps simply become shorter and higher without loss of impulsion and activity.

In collection the hind legs and hindquarters (hock and stifle joints) bend more and take more of the weight, with the hind legs stepping further underneath the horse in the direction of the centre of gravity. This in turn lightens the forehand, giving more freedom to the movements of the forelegs. When collected, the horse looks and feels as if it is taking more expressive, elevated steps. In driving, collection is required only in trot.

By training and developing the relevant muscles it is possible to increase the carrying capacity of the hindquarters. On the other hand, the forelegs, which support rather than push, can only be strengthened to a very limited degree through training. It is therefore better, and indeed necessary, to transfer some of the weight onto the quarters.

The increased flexion of the hind legs results in the neck being raised. If the carrying capacity of the hindquarters is sufficiently developed, the horse is then in a position to move in balance and self-carriage in all three gaits.

'Through'/'letting the aids through' (Durchlässigkeit)

Being 'through' or 'letting the aids through' means that the horse is prepared to accept the rider's aids obediently and without tension. It should respond to the forward-driving aids without hesitation, i.e. its hind legs should 'swing through' energetically, creating forward thrust. At the same time the rein aids should pass through, i.e. be 'allowed through' from the mouth, via the poll, neck and back, to the hindquarters, without being blocked by tension at any point.

> **Note**: The horse can be said to be 'through' or to 'let the aids through' (*durchlässig*) when it remains loose (*losgelassen*) and responds obediently, and equally on both reins, to the forward-driving and restraining aids. This quality is the hallmark of the correctly schooled horse.

A horse which can be collected at any time has attained the highest level of *Durchlässigkeit*.

Preliminary training

The lessons taught in the first few weeks form the basis not only of the preliminary stage of the young horse's training, but also of the 'loosening' (*Losgelassenheit*) or warming-up process which constitutes the first phase of each training session.

The first step is to establish a rhythm. As a starting point, the horse should be ridden in the basic form of the gait (which will vary from horse to horse) and the driver should send the horse smoothly and evenly forward, while keeping a quiet, elastic contact. Sending the horse forward does not mean chasing it along, which simply leads to hurried steps and loss of rhythm. 'Forwards' does not mean fast, i.e. a rapid tempo: it means stimulating the hind legs to propel the body actively and powerfully forward. Regularity, in all three basic gaits, takes precedence over all else.

The main causes of loss of rhythm are faults in the sequence or timing of the footfalls, for example a 'pace-like' walk or a four-time canter. In trot the commonest problems are short, irregular, tense steps, or so-called 'hovering' steps. Usually rhythm faults or loss of rhythm are caused by using too much hand and insufficient forward-driving aids, or interfering with the horse's balance by poling it up or putting it in too tightly.

Loosening exercises can be helpful, including frequent transitions and getting the horse to take the rein forward and downward, as can skilful lungeing, work under saddle, cavalletti, and possibly gymnastic jumping and riding across country.

Looseness (*Losgelassenheit*) is a central theme running through the schooling. It should never be neglected, and must be constantly checked and reinforced. Before trying to obtain looseness in the driven horse, the trainer must first ensure that the horse is happy in itself and mentally relaxed. This can be achieved through regular, sensitive care and handling, and sufficient exercise. Once the horse is 'mentally loosened', external, physical looseness comes relatively quickly.

Loosening exercises serve to warm up the muscles, tendons and joints, as well as to make the horse work more through its back. They also serve to stimulate the hind legs to engage and 'swing through' more, and to encourage the horse to stretch towards the bit and take a confident contact.

When problems arise at a later stage in the horse's schooling, the trainer should go back to the loosening exercises again. Most training faults have more than one cause and need to be looked at as a whole. Usually, however, looseness (*Losgelassenheit*) is involved in one way or another, and the horse has been driven incorrectly. The fault can take many different forms, for example tightness in the back, hind legs lacking activity, a 'dead' mouth, crookedness and leaning away from the pole.

In the preliminary training and while warming up and loosening up at other times, the horse should be driven on a **light contact**. It is with a light contact that it can most easily find its balance and begin to develop rhythm and looseness. This applies both to young and more experienced horses.

The horse should go into the reins and seek a contact with the bit in response to the forward-driving aids, and encouraged by the sensitive use of the driver's hand.

When the horse first comes onto the contact it will be with a relatively low position of the head and neck, i.e. with the mouth

Note: Rhythm (regularity and purity of the gait) and looseness (freedom from constraint) are the criteria by which every exercise should be judged.

approximately level with the point of the shoulder. This is the best position for teaching the horse to stretch and relax its neck and back muscles.

Developing the forward thrust

Developing the forward thrust or 'pushing power' involves stimulating the hind legs to work more actively and engage further underneath the horse's body towards the centre of gravity. Forward thrust is required before the carrying capacity of the hind legs can be developed, i.e. before the horse can take more weight onto its quarters.

The horse is said to be **on the contact** when it is going forward into its bridle, irrespective of the length of its frame. As the forward thrust develops and the hind legs engage further in the direction of the centre of gravity, the horse will become able and willing to bend its neck more and flex through its poll, bringing its nose closer to the vertical. If the trainer ignores this principle and attempts to force the horse into a shorter outline, he will simply block the activity of the horse's back and hind legs. Hence when judging whether or not the horse is correctly on the contact or on the bit, it is not enough to look only at the head and neck. You need to look at the whole horse, its position and carriage, and in particular the way it moves.

Unfortunately, mistakes are frequently made when teaching the horse to come onto the contact. These result in many different faults, the commonest of which are as follows:

NOSE BEHIND THE VERTICAL

Going with the nose behind the vertical is caused by using the hands too strongly. This fault may result either from a momentary mistake in applying the aids, or it may be a symptom of long-term incorrect schooling.

The only way to correct it is by driving the horse forward and at the same time yielding with the hands.

BEHIND THE CONTACT, DROPPING THE CONTACT

With this problem, not only is the horse's nose behind the vertical, but also the horse evades the action of the bit by backing off from the contact: it refuses to go into its bridle. Often, at the same time, the head is flexed from a vertebra further down the neck rather than at the poll (see 'false bend').

The first step is to re-establish the contact. The horse must learn to have confidence in the rider's hand. Skilful lungeing can also be helpful, and sending the horse actively forwards in harness, especially out of doors, or increasing the weight the horse has to pull, sometimes helps to get the horse to stretch forward onto the contact.

To correct this fault, the driver needs to be especially sensitive in his co-ordination of the driving and restraining aids. It takes a soft, elastic hand to 'push the nose forward'.

FALSE BEND

This occurs as a result of the driver trying to establish the contact by acting in a backward direction with his hands. The highest point of the neck is no longer the poll, but a point further back, usually between the third and fourth vertebrae. This is a serious fault which can only be corrected, if at all, by lengthy, systematic, knowledgeable reschooling.

To correct this fault, the trainer needs to send the horse energetically forwards while preventing rhythm faults or hurrying by elastic use of his hands, and at the same time 'giving' sufficiently with his hands to allow the neck to adopt the correct outline.

'Taking the rein forward and downward' is a good exercise for horses with this fault. The horse needs to learn all over again how to stretch its topline and go forwards onto the contact. Often if the horse goes with a false bend, or is behind the contact, this is because it has been driven in a bit which is too severe in its action, or with the reins attached too far down the cheek of the bit, giving too much leverage.

LEANING ON THE BIT

The horse seeks support from the driver's hands, using them as a 'fifth foot', and is not working sufficiently from behind. The driver needs to stimulate the hind legs to greater activity by increased use of his forward-driving aids.

Judicious 'asking' and yielding alternately with the hands, and performing frequent transitions with a sensitive hand can be effective against this fault. On no account should the driver 'offer' his hand as a support.

AGAINST THE HAND, ABOVE THE BIT

In this fault the horse's nose is well in front of the vertical. The horse will not flex at the poll, and uses the muscles on the underside of the neck to resist the hand, while at the same time stiffening and hollowing its back. If this is a long-standing fault, and the wrong muscles have been allowed to develop, lungeing with side-reins can be especially beneficial. The side-reins should be shortish at first, and then gradually lengthened. As the horse learns to stretch, the correct musculature will then gradually develop.

In some especially difficult cases, because of the conformation and the shape of the neck, when the horse is in an extended outline and yielding at the poll, its nose may be slightly behind the vertical to start with. The driver must then take special care to maintain the activity of the hind legs and to avoid making the horse short in its neck (i.e. 'pulling the horse together') by using his hands too strongly. Forcing the horse in this way would simply create tension and, since the neck is the horse's 'balancing pole', would seriously disturb the horse's balance, and make it impossible to obtain the required 'looseness'. Here again, giving the horse more weight to pull can be helpful.

The **impulsion** can be developed and improved by performing transitions from one gait, and form of the gait, to another. Special emphasis should be placed on maintaining the rhythm through the transitions, and on sensitive use of the rein aids during the downward transitions so as not to restrict the forward movement of the hind legs and prevent them from 'swinging through'.

Impulsion must not be confused with the term 'action', which simply refers to the horse's inherent ability to take expressive, ground-covering trot steps. The horse may, at the same time, be tense and hollow, and tight in its back.

If the horse is working with impulsion, the moment of suspension will be more pronounced. However, it should not be exaggerated and 'in slow motion', since this would result in incorrect **hovering steps**, which are associated with tension.

It is not only in dressage that correct contact and impulsion are essential. They enable any rider or driver to remain constantly and harmoniously in control of the horse, the tempo and the direction. As a result of impulsion, the activity of the hindquarters is increased so that the hind feet push off more energetically from the ground and the horse is able to take more efficient, ground-covering trot strides.

If the horse is working with impulsion it will respond correctly to the driving aids: that is, it will not hurry or fall onto the forehand, but will 'let the impulsion through' from behind. The development and improvement of the impulsion is of fundamental importance, and features equally in the development of the forward thrust and of the carrying power of the quarters. It is also a fundamental prerequisite for straightness and collection.

Development of the carrying capacity of the hindquarters
(Training the horse to take the weight onto the quarters)

Training aimed specifically at the developing the straightness and collection, and so getting the horse to take more weight onto the quarters, is not feasible until the forward thrust is fairly well ingrained. The rhythm in all three basic paces also needs to be established, along with the 'looseness' and the contact. The development of impulsion and straightness are essential to prepare the horse for collection and so to make it more supple and 'through'. This principles are clearly expressed in the words of Gustav Steinbrecht, a nineteenth-century classical horseman:

> *'Ride your horse forwards and position it straight'*

Although Steinbrecht is referring here to the ridden horse, these principles apply equally in driving.

Impulsion is the main criterion. Aids which act in a backward direction are always incorrect. The horse is said to be straight or straight to the track when, while working on a single track, be it straight or curved, its longitudinal axis is aligned with the track.

Preliminary work on straightness begins as soon as the young horse learns to respond to the driver's aids. However, exercises aimed specifically at developing **straightness** cannot begin until the forward thrust and impulsion have been developed, since they need to be performed with the horse going positively forwards. If, for example, the horse is crooked to the right, that is, the right hind foot follows a track outside that of the left forefoot, this means that the right hind foot is escaping sideways in order to avoid having to bend. This throws more weight onto the left shoulder, and as a result the horse tends to lean on the left rein.

On the left side the neck muscles are stiff, tense and unyielding. This side is known as the 'stiff side'. The difficult side, however, is the hollow, right side. The right hind leg escapes sideways and the horse refuses to go into the right rein. Schooling should be aimed at getting the right hind leg to step forwards straight, and underneath the body. This will result in the horse stretching forward to, and taking a contact on, the right rein. When this happens, the stiffness on the left side will disappear by itself. Ways to achieve this are as follows:

- in harness, by adjusting the length of the coupling rein, and by use of the whip;

- by corrective work on the lunge or in long reins;

- through ridden work.

Collection is achieved only through correctly structured appropriate training and through patience.

If the horse is working with impulsion, performing transitions on straight and curved tracks will improve the straightness and collection. The forward thrust increases as a result of correct use of the forward-driving aids. However, instead of 'giving' with his hand and allowing the energy to flow forwards, as in lengthening the strides, the driver uses what is more a non-yielding or 'asking' rein aid and 'catches up' the energy, which is then passed back through a supple back to the hindquarters, with the result that more weight is taken on the quarters.

So as not to restrict the forward swing of the horse's hind legs, 'catching up' the energy requires skilful, sensitive rein aids, used in conjunction with the voice and possibly the whip. Any exercise which teaches the horse to carry more weight on the quarters is a **collecting exercise**. The difference between a 'collecting' exercise and a 'collected' exercise lies in the degree of perfection with which it is performed.

As a basic principle, in between periods of collecting or straightening work the driver should push the horse actively forwards in order to preserve the **purity of the gait**. The quality of the collection training can be judged by sending the horse forward from a collected into an extended trot, and assessing the correctness and rhythm of the gait. If during the extension the horse leans on the bit, loses rhythm, resists or tightens, this means that the collection training has been incorrectly performed or the horse has been pushed too hard. If, on the other hand, the extended trot is characterised by regular, expressive strides, this is a sign that the collection training has been carried out correctly. The horse is prepared to lengthen its frame in keeping with the longer, more ground-covering action and go forwards with looseness, rhythm and impulsion while maintaining a light contact.

In the transition back to collection, if the horse has been correctly schooled, the impulsion from the extended trot will 'carry through' into the collected trot, resulting in more elevated, cadenced steps.

Cadence means that the moment of suspension is more clearly marked. At the same time the hind legs must 'swing through' and engage well underneath the horse otherwise incorrect hovering steps will occur, which are a sign of tension and stiffness in the back.

The duration of the collection training or collected work depends on how fit the horse is. If overdone, it simply leads to tension and resistance.

The carriage of the head and neck is directly related to the collection: i.e. the head is raised proportionately to the degree of collection or, in dressage parlance, **relatively raised**.

Hence a horse which is 'on the bit' but in a longish outline, and carrying less weight on its hindquarters, will carry its head and neck lower. As the horse takes more weight onto its quarters, i.e. as the collection increases, the forehand becomes lighter. The hindquarters are lowered as a result of the increased flexion, making the horse look higher in front and so slightly 'uphill'. With correct training this carriage develops naturally. Raising the head mainly by use of the hands is incorrect. The head carriage is no longer related to the degree of engagement: in dressage parlance the head and neck are said to be raised **absolutely**, as opposed to relatively. Instead of the horse being in self-carriage, the driver is supporting the head and neck with his hands and the activity of the hind legs is restricted because the horse is not working correctly through its back. If, on the other hand, the carrying capacity of the hindquarters is correctly developed, the horse will be able to move in balance and self-carriage in all the gaits.

'Letting the aids through' (*Durchlässigkeit*) is the result of correct gymnastic schooling, or 'gymnasticising'. If the horse exhibits *Durchlässigkeit*, this is conclusive proof that the training has been correct. 'Letting the aids through' is closely related to, and interconnected with, the other elements of the 'Scales of Training':

- It allows the rhythm to be maintained reliably in all three gaits, and particularly in the transitions.

- Only if the horse moves with 'looseness' (*Losgelassenheit*) can the energy from the hindquarters pass forward through the horse's body. It also allows the restraining aids to act, via the mouth, poll, neck and back, on the hindquarters.

- Any problems in the contact, that is, unsteadiness or stiffness in the connection between the rider's hand and the horse's mouth, will interfere directly with the horse's ability to 'let the aids through'.

- A horse which works with impulsion, which is supple through its back and so 'swings through' with its hind legs, will be better able to 'let the aids through'.

- Not until the horse becomes straighter can it perform the half-halts equally on both reins, and at the same time go more positively into the contact in response to the driver's forward-driving aids, without its hind legs escaping to the side.

- This, in its turn, is absolutely essential for collection, and consequently for the correct raising of the head and neck which results from it.

- If the horse responds correctly to the exercises in collection by stepping forward more, and with both hind legs equally, in the direction of the centre of gravity, and by taking more weight on its quarters as required, this is an indication that it has achieved a high degree of *Durchlässigkeit*.

Dressage schooling is an essential requirement for all driving horses.

Training in walk

At the beginning of its training, the young horse needs to learn to walk quietly and get used to the driver's forward-driving aids. As a general rule, for the first few months the driver should simply keep a light contact with the horse's mouth in walk, otherwise it can all too easily become irregular. The driver should allow the natural nodding movement of the horse's head and neck so as not to restrict the walk.

Asking the horse to come onto the contact too early in walk, or 'placing' the horse's head with the hands can seriously affect the regularity and length of the strides, as well as leading to tension. These faults can be very difficult to correct in later training. Incorrect use of the forward-driving aids, as well as the restraining aids, will spoil the walk.

All horses, and not just youngsters, should be walked, with the driver maintaining a light contact, for 10–15 minutes at the beginning of every training session before starting the trot work. This helps to make them mentally relaxed, and ensures that the joints, tendons and muscles are warmed up gradually.

The horse should frequently be given the opportunity to walk on a long rein or a loose rein in between periods of trot. This makes it easier for the young horse to get used to the unfamiliar work, and in the case of older horses, it provides an opportunity to relax mentally and physically in between the different elements of the training session.

Training in trot

For the first few weeks the young horse should simply be allowed to trot calmly, in the trot which comes most naturally to it, without needing to put much weight into the traces, until it can move with looseness and has found its balance to some extent in this gait. The horse should be driven forwards, but without hurrying, on straight lines and gentle turns. This teaches it to accept the forward-driving aids.

Being driven forwards onto a soft contact and through a swinging back serves to develop the forward thrust of the quarters. Trot is the gait in which it is easiest for the young horse to learn to take a contact.

Once the rhythm and the contact are established, the driver can try briefly increasing the strides, and then decreasing them again through gentle half-halts. It is important not to ask for too much at this stage: a few lengthened strides are enough.

Training in canter

Canter training is only necessary if the horse is to be used for cross-country and obstacle-driving competitions. The aim is to get the horse to canter reliably 'on the aids' and to remain under control at all times. Canter work should be introduced on the lunge and under saddle. For the next stage it is a good idea to drive the horse next to an experienced cross-country horse.

Upward and downward **transitions** both from one gait to another and from one form of the trot to another, teach the horse to use its hind legs more actively in response to the driver's forward-driving aids and to swing through its back.

The driver should not ask for the transition too abruptly, for fear of upsetting its balance. If, to start with, it takes the horse a few moments to understand and react to the driver's aids, and it is then praised, it will pick it up more quickly than if force is used. Harsh driving and restraining aids will simply upset the horse and cause tension. The same principles apply when riding transitions to halt.

When **driving turns and circles**, the trainer should start with large circles and gentle curves such as single shallow loops in from the track on the long side and three or four-loop serpentines through the whole school. Circles should be no less than 20m in diameter.

New exercises should always be performed for short periods at first, and followed by driving the horse actively forwards to re-establish the impulsion and looseness. The trainer should be satisfied if the horse satisfies the new demands only partially to start with. Making the horse more obedient, and more supple and 'through' to the driver's aids is of greater value than getting it to perform the exercise correctly but mechanically.

During the basic training, the aim of the riding-in or 'loosening' phase of the lesson is to get the horse to meet certain essential criteria, which will then form the basis for, and underlie the main or 'working phase' of the lesson, during which the new material is then slowly and gradually introduced. Hence during the main part of the lesson the horse should still be allowed to 'take the rein forward and downward' at regular intervals as a test of the rhythm, looseness, contact and impulsion. The 'relaxation and recovery' phase at the end of the lesson should always be long enough to allow the horse to return to its stable relaxed and in a positive frame of mind.

Once the necessary degree of suppleness and *Durchlässigkeit* has been achieved in its basic training, the trainer can start work on the more **advanced straightening** and collecting exercises (**collection**). Frequently alternating between easier and more difficult work, and between different forms of the gait, will help to keep the horse interested and happy in its work, and to maintain the impulsion. It is a mistake to perform only collected work for extended periods with young horses. Only by driving the horse forward out of the collection can the trainer ensure that it is always prepared to step forwards, with both hind feet equally, in the direction of its centre of gravity and carry its body-weight forwards.

The periods of collected work can be gradually increased as the horse becomes fitter and the musculature more developed. Trying to do too much too soon leads to tension and possible resistance, and never gives the desired result.

The **exercises** should be progressive. Often, through ignorance, horses are asked to do things they are not ready for because they are not supple enough and have not received the necessary gymnastic training. They can then only perform these exercises in a tense, constrained fashion. The first priority is to ensure that the horse understands the basic aids which will be used in the new exercise. The trainer must use his 'feel' and knowledge to decide when the horse is in a position to understand the new demands and when it is ready to 'offer' the new exercise of its own accord.

> **Note**: Throughout training, the exercises are not an end in themselves, but merely a gauge of the success of the training so far and of the suppleness (*Durchlässigkeit*) of the horse.

If the horse responds obediently and without stiffening to the forward-driving and restraining aids, it will have no problem coping with the basic dressage exercises. These exercises are not an end in themselves, but should fall into the driver's lap 'like a ripe fruit' if the training is correct and as the suppleness increases. If misunderstandings arise between horse and driver during the training, it will almost always be necessary to lower the demands and go back and check the basic training. Often the horse's education has not followed the 'Scales of Training': one step on the ladder has been omitted so that something is missing from the overall picture of the 'correctly schooled horse'. The horse will not then be in a position to do what is asked of it.

It usually takes about two years to complete the horse's basic training. Depending on the horse, however, this phase may sometimes last longer.

> **Note**: Only if the trainer constantly bears in mind the concepts which form the basis of the training will he be in a position to produce a horse which is supple and 'lets the aids through'.

TEAMS, TANDEMS, ETC. ('MULTIPLES')

TYPES OF TURNOUT

This section deals with various turnouts other than singles or pairs. The names of the different types of turnout, which are distinguished by the number of horses and their positions, are as follows:

- Four-in-hand (team)
- Five-in-hand
- Six-in-hand
- Tandem
- Random
- Unicorn
- Troika

FOUR-IN-HAND OR TEAM

A four-in-hand consists of four horses harnessed in pairs. The two horses immediately in front of the vehicle are known as the wheelers or wheel horses, and the two in front of them as the leaders or lead horses. As with pairs, two styles of turnout are possible depending on the type of harness used: i.e. full collar or breastcollar. To be correct, the turnout should consist of horses which are as far as possible evenly matched. The leaders should be slightly finer and have more quality and presence than the wheelers. The vehicle should be the right weight for the horses: it should not be too heavy, but neither should it be too light.

SIX-IN-HAND

A six-in-hand consists of three pairs of horses harnessed one pair in front of the other to a heavy, sufficiently high vehicle. The horses should be 'together' in their movements, and they should be on the bit and should 'let the aids through'.

TANDEM

A tandem consists of two horses harnessed one in front of the other. The 'shaft horse' or wheeler, i.e. the one immediately in font of the vehicle, may be of a heavier type. The leader should be finer and particularly forward-going. A well-balanced two-wheeled tandem-cart is the ideal vehicle for driving a tandem. As in driving a team, it is important that the driver's seat should be high up. The 'shaft horse' should preferably wear full collar harness. The leader may wear breastcollar harness, though full collar is also acceptable.

RANDEM

A randem is made up of three horses harnessed one in front of the other. The type of harness and the choice of a vehicle are the same as for a tandem.

UNICORN

The unicorn is a type of turnout not often seen. It consists of a pair, with a third horse harnessed in front as in a tandem. Any vehicle which is suitable for a pair can be used for a unicorn.

HARNESS AND EQUIPMENT FOR TEAMS, TANDEMS, ETC.

[In the UK far more alternatives, both in types of vehicles and types of harness, are in common use, for example fixed rein terrets or 'roger rings' as opposed to the drop terrets mentioned here – Translator.]

For these turnouts, certain additional items of equipment are necessary, both on the harness and on the vehicle. Otherwise what has been said about pairs also applies here.

FOUR-IN-HAND

Irrespective of whether the horses are wearing breastcollar or full collar harness, the following extra items are necessary for the wheelers:

- One bridle terret buckled from the back into the throatlatch on the outside (i.e. away from the pole) of each wheel horse's bridle. The lead reins (leader's reins) pass through these terrets.

- On team harness, one centre terret on each of the wheelers' pads (in the position occupied by the bearing rein hook on pairs harness). These are also for the lead reins, and make it easy to tell which rein is which.

The pole on a team vehicle must have a hook for the attachment of the lead bars. This hook or 'crab' has a leather strap fastened across the opening to prevent the wheelers' bits being caught on it.

It is even more important with a team that the pole head can turn, so that if one horse falls the pole head will turn with it and help prevent injury and damage.

The harness used for the leaders is similar to pairs harness. The normal Achenbach pair reins are not suitable for the wheelers of a team because the coupling buckles are too close to the hand, and with some of the rein-holds used for teams the buckles finish up actually in the hand.

Team wheeler reins depend on the type of vehicle. The correct measurement for the outside rein is 2.45m from the bit buckle to the middle hole. The coupling rein should be 2.57m, i.e. 12cm longer. The total length of the outside rein should be 4.2–4.5m.

On the lead reins the middle hole is 2.15m from the bit buckle on the outside rein, and the coupling reins are 2.27m long so that the couplings are well clear of the wheelers. The total length of the outside lead reins is 7.2–7.5m. On the lead reins the last splice (join) must be the same distance from the bit on each rein so that the reins can be adjusted accurately before mounting.

With Achenbach team reins it is possible to drive a four-in-hand correctly at all times. The leaders are attached to the vehicle by means of the lead bars (a main bar and

Tandem

two single bars). The whip used with a team is different from that used with a pair. With full collar harness it is stylistically correct to use a bow-top whip. The length of the stick should be such that the driver can apply the whip level with the pad (when using the whip on the wheelers the thong is furled and it is the loop hanging down, or 'double thong' as it is called, which touches the horse). The thong, when extended, should be long enough for the driver to reach the leaders without having to lean forward. More on this subject can be found in the section 'The team whip and its use'.

Because teams, tandems, etc. are longer than pairs, the driver needs to sit higher to be able to see what is going on. For this reason, vehicles designed for this type of turnout are equipped with a sloping, wedge-shaped cushion, which must be securely attached to the seat.

SIX-IN-HAND

Harness and equipment for a six-in-hand is similar to that used for a four-in-hand. The total length of the lead reins is between 10.2m and 10.5m. The outside rein is 2.15m from the bit to the middle hole, and the coupling rein 2.27m. Between the middle pair of horses, the 'swing pair', there is an additional pole, the 'swing pole', which is attached to the wheelers' pole hook below the main bar. The swing pole is carried by the swing horses by means of elasticated pole bearers which buckle onto the inside trace buckles. Like the wheel pole, the swing pole has a crab, and rings for the attachment of the pole straps. The leaders are attached to this pole by means of the lead bars, which should be as light as possible. To enable the reins to be told apart, there is a double terret on each of the leader's pads, so that the lead horses' and swing horses' reins go through separate rings.

TANDEM

Basically, tandem harness consists of two sets of single harness which have been modified or added to in parts. The leader is attached to the wheeler, or shaft horse, either by so-called 'long traces' or by normal single harness traces and double bars or 'tandem bars'. Bars are recommended on technical grounds.

The wheeler should wear collar harness if possible, and the tugs should be of the same length as for a single. The trace buckles should have an eye on the lower edge for the attachment of the 'long traces', or of the short traces which are connected to the first of the two 'tandem bars'. The weight of the bars is supported by a short chain attached at one end to the first bar, and at the other to a ring at the bottom of the wheeler's hames. To prevent the traces sliding over the horse's back in the turns, the leader's pad is constructed differently from the pad used in single harness. It can be narrower, and it has no tugs. Also, it has loops or slots through which the traces are passed. These either form part of the backband, or are sewn on separately.

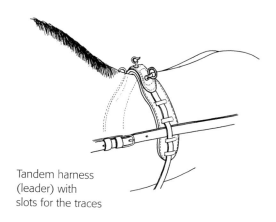

Tandem harness
(leader) with
slots for the traces

To provide separation for the four reins, the wheeler's pad is fitted with two double terrets. The wheeler's bridle has rein terrets like those used with a team. The wheeler should always wear a breeching, but care must be taken to ensure that there are no strap ends or tongues of buckles for the lead reins to get caught on.

The vehicle of choice for this type of turnout is a high tandem cart. However, it is important that the vehicle is balanced. A tandem cart with the centre of gravity too far forward or back, i.e. which is nose- or tail-heavy, is tiring for the wheel horse and unsafe for the driver.

RANDEM

The wheeler of a randem should always wear full collar harness. As with a tandem, a breeching should be used. The lead horse also wears a full collar. Both the lead horse and the centre horse are attached by means of 'tandem bars'. The use of long traces instead of bars has the disadvantage that they hang down, especially in the turns, and the horse may get a foot over the trace. With a randem the length of the lead reins is 10.2–10.5m. A tandem cart is a good vehicle for use with a randem.

UNICORN

All three horses in a unicorn should wear the same type of harness. The horse out in front (the leader) should be attached to a light lead bar hooked onto the pole. Tandem lead reins can be used for the leader, and are passed through terrets on the inside of the wheelers' bridles.

DRIVING TEAMS, TANDEMS, ETC.

To be able to control a team, the driver must first be able to drive a single and a pair safely. Most of what has been said about pairs also serves as a foundation for driving teams and tandems.

The basic rule that the reins must never be allowed to slide through the driver's hand is of particular importance with teams, tandems, etc. If, during his training, the driver has not practised making delicate adjustments to team reins on the 'driving apparatus', he will not be in a position to line up the lead horses exactly with the wheelers or vice versa, or to regulate the distribution of the work. These skills are essential for correct team driving.

Driving should not be considered simply as a functional skill or a means of transport. Like riding, it is an art, the aim of which is to bring the horses to a high level of schooling. The driver's aim is not only to make the horses' task of pulling the vehicle as easy as possible. It is first and foremost to produce horses which are obedient, which 'let the aids through' and yield at the poll without resistance, and which move with elastic impulsion and a swinging back, more or less collected depending on the situation, and with a soft mouth and the correct flexion. The driver should feel that he is in harmony with the horses, and that he and they are 'pulling together' as it were.

This harmony is a particularly creditable achievement in driving, because the driver does not have such close contact with the horse as a rider and so there are fewer kinds of aids he can use. The means the driver has at his disposal are the rein aids (the use of a soft, resisting or yielding hand, and the different rein holds) and the whip, voice and brake as required. Driving, particularly with teams, tandems, etc., requires a good understanding of the horses, a logical mind and quick reactions.

PUTTING TO AND TAKING OUT A FOUR-IN-HAND

The same harnessing-up procedure as for a pair is used, except that a bridle terret is buckled to the back of the throatlatch buckle on the outside of each leader's bridle. First the wheelers are put to, in the same way as described for pairs. Then the leaders are stood in front of the wheelers, the throatlatches are done up and the coupling reins attached to the bits. The reins are then passed through the wheelers' bridle and pad terrets, and the ends buckled together before tucking them under the point strap of the pad with the wheeler reins. The rest of the procedure is the same as for pairs.

As an additional safeguard against the traces coming off, a safety strap can be fitted on the end of each swingle tree. When performing the final check before mounting, the driver should ensure that the strap from the crab to the end of the pole has been fastened.

The horses are taken out in the reverse order to that in which they are put in. However, with a team, the driver must never attempt either operation on his own: there must always be at least one assistant present.

TAKING UP THE REINS OF A FOUR-IN-HAND

The reins are taken up as follows. The folded reins are taken out from under the point strap on the pad and laid across the left forearm from the back. They are arranged in the following order along the arm from elbow to hand: LL, RL, LW, RW. The correct amount of rein is then measured out on the wheel reins, and they are transferred to the left hand with only the middle finger between then – unlike the basic position with pair reins. The right wheel rein lies between the middle finger and the ring finger, and the left wheel rein between the middle finger and the index finger.

The driver then takes a light contact with the leaders' mouths on the lead reins, with the right lead rein held in his right hand. He then measures out the lead reins in the same way as the wheel reins. Unlike with the wheel reins, the position of the coupling buckles cannot be taken as a gauge when measuring out the lead reins, so the driver must judge their length by the position of the splice (the nearest one in front of his hand when he is driving). The left splice should be 5cm in front of the right one (the driver sits on the right-hand side of the vehicle). Once measured out, the lead reins are transferred from the right hand to the left, with the index finger between them. The right lead rein is then on top of the left wheel rein between the middle finger and the index finger, with the left lead rein over the index finger. Before the driver moves back to mount, he should take a contact with the horses' mouths on both of the left reins by making a loop with the left lead rein between his thumb and index finger, and then with the left wheel rein under his left index finger. As he moves back to mount, he gradually lets the loops out as required. The method for mounting and sitting down is the same as for pairs.

HOLDING THE REINS OF A FOUR-IN-HAND

The reins are held in either the **basic position** or the **standard position**. The schooling position described for pairs is not used with multiples. In the **basic position** all four reins are held together in the left hand. They must be held securely so that they cannot slip or be moved, except when adjusted intentionally by the right hand (in turns etc.).

In the basic position, the lead reins are separated by the index finger and the wheel reins by the middle finger, with the right lead rein lying on top of the left wheel rein between the index finger and the middle finger of the driver's left hand.

In the **standard position** the right hand, which is holding the whip, is placed just in

Basic position with four-in-hand reins

l.l.

r.l.

l.w.

r.w.

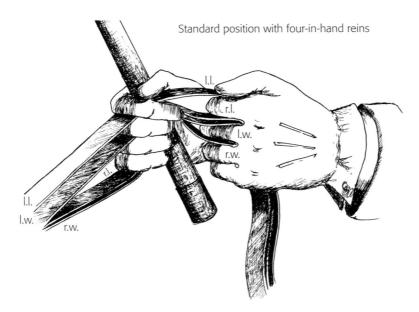

Standard position with four-in-hand reins

front of the left hand, with the little finger and the ring finger gripping the right reins (right lead, right wheel), the middle finger between the two left reins, and the thumb and index finger securing the left lead rein. The right hand can then close on the reins and take the strain off the left hand, without the left hand having to be taken off the reins.

The ends of the reins hang down to the left of the driver's left thigh.

SHORTENING AND LENGTHENING THE REINS AND KEEPING THE HORSES IN LINE IN A FOUR-IN-HAND

To **lengthen** all four reins by the same amount, the right hand closes on the reins in the standard position and pulls all the reins forward by the required amount through the left hand, which opens slightly to let them through. The left hand then closes again, and the right hand moves back up the reins until it is just in front of the left hand again.

Shortening all four reins simultaneously is performed in the same way as with a pair. The reins may be shortened:

- by a few centimetres

- by a lot

- temporarily.

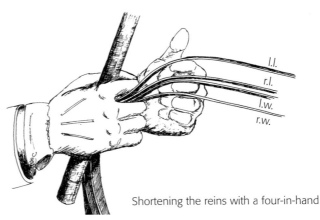

Shortening the reins with a four-in-hand

If the leaders are too much or insufficiently in draught, only the lead reins should be shortened or lengthened. Since the right lead rein lies on top of the left wheel rein in the left hand, before the length of the lead reins is adjusted, the right lead rein must first be placed on top of the index finger. To achieve this, the index finger is pulled out backwards from between the reins and then pushed underneath the right lead rein. The right hand then grasps the two lead reins, which are now lying on top of each other, and pushes them back or pulls them forward through the left hand, depending on whether they are required to be shortened or lengthened. When the adjustment is complete, the index finger returns to its former position between the two lead reins.

Shortening both wheel reins together, can be achieved either:

• by shortening all four reins and then lengthening the lead reins again, or

• by first lengthening the lead reins, and then shortening all four reins.

The method chosen depends on the extent to which the horses are in draught.

Lengthening both wheel reins together is achieved either:

• by lengthening all four reins, and then shortening the lead reins again, or

• by first shortening the lead reins, and then lengthening all four reins.

Shortening individual reins is only possible in the case of reins which run singly through the hand, i.e. the left lead rein and the right wheel rein, which are known as the 'correcting reins'. Since the right lead rein and the left wheel rein lie on top of each other between the index and middle fingers, no attempt should be made to adjust them individually.

Lengthening and shortening the left lead rein or the right wheel rein is performed from the standard position, with the right hand being used to lengthen or shorten the left lead rein. If the leaders are too far over to the left, the left lead rein is lengthened until they are straight again. Then if the lead reins are too long, they are shortened.

If the wheelers are too far over to the left, the right wheel rein is shortened. If the wheel reins are then too short, first all four reins are lengthened, and then the two lead reins are shortened by the desired amount. If the leaders are too far over to the right, the left lead rein is shortened. If the traces are then too slack, both lead reins are lengthened.

If the wheelers are too far over to the right, the right wheel rein is lengthened. If all the reins have become too long, they are shortened all together by the required amount.

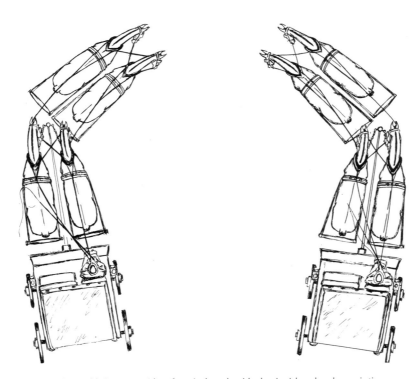

Right and left turns with a four-in-hand, with the inside wheeler pointing towards the space between the leaders, i.e. 'going into the gap'

TURNS WITH A FOUR-IN-HAND

[Some of the comments apply only when driving on the right-hand side of the road.]

In all turns with a team, the driver must always special attention to the traffic or, when driving in the exercise area, to other users such as pedestrians, riders or drivers. When driving on the roads, the relevant signals must be given, by the groom or passenger if necessary, or by the groom or passenger getting down to direct the traffic.

When coming into a turn the trot tempo should be slowed down to suit the radius of the turn and the ground surface. A tight right-hand turn is always driven at a walk. To pull out or cross over to the left-hand side of the road, the right hand takes hold of the left lead and wheel reins about 15cm in front of the right hand, with the middle finger separating them. The left hand then moves underneath the right, so yielding the right reins. To cross back over to the right, the opposite aids are used.

When driving turns with a team, the leaders must not be in draught. If the leaders are pulling the vehicle, or are even partially in draught, the vehicle will turn too sharply, i.e. cut the corner, so that the turn is incorrect. It is always the wheelers who determine the course of the vehicle, and the leaders must not be allowed to prevent

Making a loop in a right turn (corner)

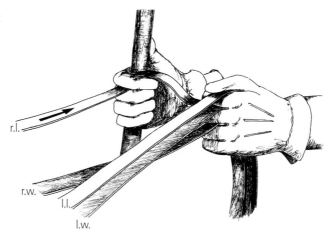

r.l.

r.w.
l.l.
l.w.

> **Note**: When making a loop, the right hand must always bring the loop **to** the rein hand (i.e. the left hand) rather than the rein hand going towards the right hand.

them doing so by interfering with their control over the pole. During the turn, the inside wheeler should point towards the space between the two leaders: in German this is called 'going into the gap' or 'towards the skylight'.

To drive a left-hand turn (corner), the driver first slows the tempo (at the same time using the brake) and ensures that the road is clear. For the inside horse to be able to 'go into the gap' and pull the vehicle correctly round the corner, the driver needs to adjust the position of his rein hand to the right or left (i.e. 'into' or 'out of' the turn) to keep the wheelers following in the tracks of the leaders.

When the leaders' heads have arrived at the point where the left turn is to begin, the driver takes hold of the left lead rein between the index finger and the middle finger of the right hand at a point about 15–20cm in front of the left hand, 'feels' the horses' mouths, and then makes a loop with this rein under the thumb of his left hand. If necessary the driver can also make a small loop on the outside wheel rein (this is called an 'opposition point') to keep the wheelers from falling in.

A loop which is too big can always be made smaller as required, but a too small loop cannot be made larger. If, when the rein has been looped, the horses start to turn too sharply, this can only be corrected by adjusting the length of the reins. Resisting on the outside rein will simply make the horses turn their heads outwards, i.e. cause them to have the 'wrong bend'.

For a right turn (corner), the horses should be brought back to a walk. It may be necessary to shorten the reins. The driver then takes hold of the right lead rein about 20cm in front of the left hand, and makes a loop with it under the index finger. If necessary, the left hand can go 'into the turn'. The loop is let out as required. The left hand then returns to its original position.

Left and right 'U' turns ('about turns') should be avoided since they place a lot of strain on the horses. However, they should be learned and practised on the 'driving apparatus' since they can crop up in competitions.

REIN-BACK

To obtain a smooth, controlled rein-back with a team, the driver needs to practise regularly with a pair. Before the rein-back, the lead reins should first be lengthened, and then all four reins shortened. The driver then brings his hand back as far as is necessary to get the horses to step backwards with even strides. Care must be taken to ensure that they do not deviate from a straight line. To make the horses go forward again, the driver moves his hand forward in the direction of the horses' mouths and lengthens the reins. It is a good idea to apply the brake on completion of the rein-back.

THE TEAM WHIP AND ITS USE

The driver of a four-in-hand must be in a position to give the necessary whip aids to the leaders as well as the wheelers. For him to be able to do so, the whip must be correctly constructed and of the right length, and he must be practised in its use. A dummy horse should be used for the first lessons in the use of the whip, and the driver should sit high enough off the ground to be able to practise catching and furling the thong. To prevent it getting caught in the wheels, hitting passers-by, or upsetting the other horses in the team, the thong of a team whip must be caught and wound round the stick when it is not being used on the leaders. Catching and furling the thong is easier if the stick is stiff and has knots on the top part on which the thong can gain a purchase.

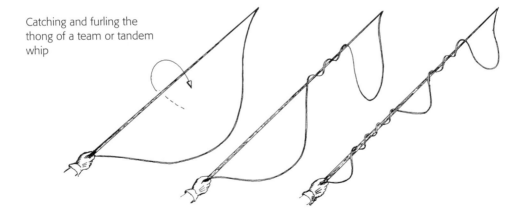

Catching and furling the thong of a team or tandem whip

Before catching the thong, the lash at the end of it should be held under the hand on the handpiece of the whip, so that the thong is hanging down in a large loop. The thong is then caught by holding it slightly above the horizontal and describing a reversed 'S' shape in the air with it, from bottom left to top right. At the same time the hand turns so that the driver can see his thumb nail during the first half of the 'S', and the other

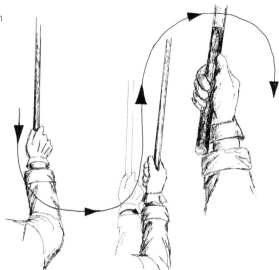

Hand movements used in catching and furling the thong

four nails and his thumb during the second half. The arm should be extended as much as possible.

The movement begins slowly, with the whip slightly below the horizontal. About half way through the 'S' (see illustration) the speed starts to build up, and then the movement finishes abruptly at the top, when the hand suddenly stops, leaving the thong to wind itself round the stick. The hand must turn as described during the movement. The driver must never try to catch the thong by 'following it', i.e. moving the stick sharply forward towards it: the thong must swing towards and onto the stick, and wind itself around it twice in each direction. When the thong is furled as shown in the illustration, the right (whip) hand is placed next to the left hand in front of the stomach so that the driver can catch hold of the thong with the left hand. He then moves his right hand to the right, away from his body, so that his left hand, which remains stationary, pulls the lower thread of the thong off the stick, but without disturbing the top part. With the end of the thong held in the left hand, the driver then swings the stick around its longitudinal axis so that the main loop swings around the stick without unwinding the part already twisted around it. The driver then uses his fingers to turn the stick in his right hand so that the thong is wound around the stick. The end result is that the thong is twisted in the same direction all the way down the stick. When a team whip is caught and furled, the end of the lash is secured under the thumb. The loop which is left hanging down at the top end (the 'double thong' as it is called) serves as a whip for use on the wheelers.

> **Note**: Correct, accurate whip handling is only possible with frequent practice.

To use the whip on the leaders, the driver first points the stick slightly downwards and to the right and swings it round from his wrist to unwind the thong. He then releases the lash from under his thumb and, putting the end of the stick on his right thigh, slides his hand down to the bottom of the handpiece.

To use the whip on the right (off) leader, the driver uses his whole arm, from the shoulder, to describe a circular movement with the whip in the opposite direction to the wheels, and lays the whip in the horse as far forward as possible. To use the whip on the left (near) leader, the driver first swings the thong over to the left of the horses with a twist of his wrist, taking care not to disturb them. He then describes a circle to the left (again in the opposite direction to the wheels) and lays the thong well forward on the left leader.

The whip should not be brought back immediately, which would cause the thong to catch the wheelers. If, when bringing it back, the driver turns the bow of the whip slowly across and above the horses from left to right, the thong will fall on the driver's right thigh or under his right arm. It can then be picked up with the thumb and index finger of the right hand and held against the stick. The right hand then moves over towards the left thumb, which pulls the thong through the right hand to the end (the driver must make absolutely certain that this does not interfere with the adjustment of the reins). The thong is then ready to be caught and furled again.

When giving whip aids, the driver must always use his whole arm. Using the wrist only to apply the whip or bring it back is incorrect, and causes it to become caught on the harness or on trees.

DRIVING A TEAM WITH THE REINS IN BOTH HANDS ('TWO-HANDED')

In recent years, driving a team with the reins in both hands has become acceptable for cross-country and obstacle driving. This system is now the one most widely used in driving competitions because it makes it possible to drive more accurately through cones and obstacles.

It is still the 'Achenbach reins' which are used with this method of rein handling, except that, because of the risk of them getting caught in the terrets, there are no coupling buckles on the lead reins. Instead, the rein billets are made longer so that an adjustment of up to three or four holes can be made directly at the end of the reins. Also, two extra buckles are fitted using additional holes in the hand parts of the lead and wheel reins. The buckles should be rounded, i.e. without corners, since they are designed to be in the hand or just behind it. Another way is to use two shoe-laces to tie the reins together. The holes in the reins should be positioned so that when the driver sits upright and has a contact with the horses' mouths, there is a straight line from his (slightly bent) elbow through his hand and the reins. The driver must ensure that the leaders are not in draught in the cross-country obstacles (marathon hazards), or dur-

Driving 'two-handed'

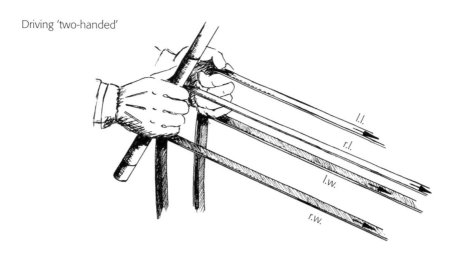

ing the obstacle driving. When driving the roads and tracks the reins can be adjusted so that the leaders are in draught, which will take some of the strain off the wheelers. It is important to buckle or tie the reins together to prevent them slipping out of the driver's hand. The buckles are either in the hands or just behind when the hands are in an upright position. Both the left reins (lead and wheel reins) are held in the left hand, and both right reins in the right hand, with the right hand also holding the whip. The lead reins run between the thumb and forefinger, with the wheel reins under the little finger.

When driving turns it is important that both hands remain upright and together in order to be able to loop the reins. To loop the lead rein, for example in a left turn, the

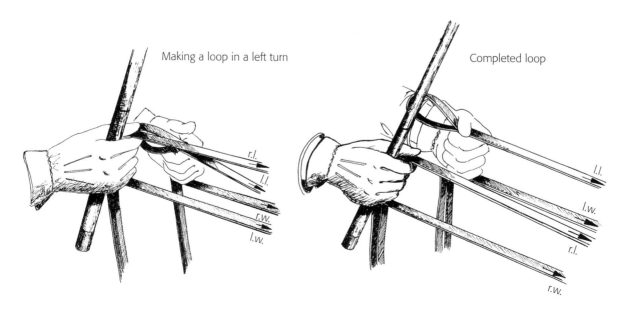

Making a loop in a left turn

Completed loop

driver takes hold of the left rein with his right thumb and forefinger only a short distance in front of the left hand, and by turning his hand backwards, places the rein under his left thumb. This action is repeated as often as necessary, depending on the radius of the turn. The size of the loop can be increased at any point. The outside hand gives as required, again depending on the radius of the turn. If it goes too far forward, so that the reins are slack, the contact on the outside of the horses' mouths will be lost and they will fall into the turn. The loop is gradually let out by slowly lifting the thumb on completion of the turn. Right-hand turns are performed in exactly in the same way but using the opposite hands.

The whip is used on the wheelers by lowering the right hand in such a way that it does not disturb the horses' mouths. To use the whip on the leaders, the right reins are transferred to the left hand, where they are held exactly in the same position as the left reins. This leaves the driver's right hand free to give the whip aids to the leaders.

When driving with the reins in both hands, the 'asking' and yielding aids are the basis of the system just as they are when driving 'Achenbach-style'. Only a skilful driver who has mastered the Achenbach system will be able, in the marathon and obstacle phases of a modern competition, to achieve success and drive safely, reliably, and with minimum strain on the horses.

> **Note**: The Achenbach system remains the definitive system for basic schooling and team dressage.

TANDEM AND UNICORN

The same rein holds and positions which are used when driving a four-in-hand are also used with tandems and unicorns, though scaled to their particular requirements. However, tandem driving presents particular problems because the reins are much closer together, which makes it more difficult for the driver to tell, by looking at them, which is which.

For a left turn, from the standard position, the driver releases the left reins and slides the right hand forward 10cm along the right reins. Holding the two right reins as one, the driver then, by turning his hand, picks up the left lead rein with the thumb and index finger of the right hand and makes a loop with it for the left turn. The loop must be made in several stages, and the left thumb should not be allowed to come in front of the right one to grip the rein.

For a right turn, both lead reins must be shortened. If the traces are slack, this ensures that the leader cannot pull the vehicle round. The driver takes hold of all four reins with his right hand about 15cm in front of his left hand, and then releases the left lead rein and increases his contact on the left wheel rein. He then turns his left hand forwards and anticlockwise, and moves it forward slightly in a yielding action. This lengthens the left lead rein and causes the leader to turn to the right.

In tandem driving, preparing the horses for the turn is even more important than for a four- or six-in-hand driving. Failure to do so may result in the leader spinning round to face the driver! Driving a tandem is made considerably easier by judicious use of harness and harnessing techniques. Long traces, as opposed to bars, have the disadvantage that the leader pulls the vehicle across into the turn if the lead reins have not been shortened sufficiently. There is also a risk that, if the traces are too slack, the leader will get a foot over them. Tandem bars are preferable, though they do have the slight disadvantage that the weight is taken mostly on the wheeler's neck, and they can bang against its forelegs when going downhill. A good, experienced four-in-hand driver will be able to 'tune in' and quickly develop a 'feel' for tandem driving, and by adapting his aids should be able to make himself understood. The fact that the reins are closer together should not cause him a problem, since right and left turns are still made by looping the reins.

DRIVING A SIX-IN-HAND AND A RANDEM

The best way to hold the reins with a six-in-hand is the same as with a four-in-hand, with the addition of an extra pair of reins. The lead reins of a six-in-hand lie on top of those of the swing pair, i.e. left lead on top of left swing and right lead on top of right swing. Underneath right swing is left wheel, and below these, on its own, is right wheel.

With six horses to control, the driver's workload is particularly high. He must be constantly checking that the horses are correctly aligned, and that the leaders and swing pair are sufficiently 'in work' to make the traces taut, but no more. On no account should the leaders and swing pair pull the vehicle unless extra traction is required, for example when going uphill or in heavy going.

If the leaders are too much in draught, the driver makes a small loop in his left hand with each of the lead reins, and then lets it slip through behind his hand.

If the swing pair is too much in draught, the driver puts his index finger underneath the top four reins (leaders and swing pair) and shortens them, as with a four-in hand. He then takes his finger out again and lengthens the lead reins.

If the leaders are insufficiently in draught, the lead reins are pulled forward individually by the right hand to lengthen them.

If the swing pair are insufficiently in draught, the lead and swing reins are lengthened, and then the lead reins are shortened again. It is up to the driver to decide whether to use the whip.

In a right turn it is especially important that the wheeler is going forward reliably into its collar, and that it pulls the vehicle into and through the turn. However, the driver can prepare for the turn by lengthening the right wheel rein one or two centimetres beforehand. Since the lead and swing reins lie on top of each other, it is not always easy to manipulate the lead reins. Placing the right lead rein on top of the left index finger beforehand will make it easier to get hold of the correct rein when required.

To begin the turn, the driver makes a sufficiently large loop with the right lead rein with his right hand, and places it under the left index finger. Then, immediately afterwards, he makes a loop with right swing rein, and a second loop with the right lead rein. When looping the reins, the left hand moves 'into the turn', i.e. towards the driver's right hip, to prevent the wheelers turning early, and the leaders falling into the turn. The loops are released individually after the turn, or as required, with the right hand assisting. Since right-hand turns are always driven in walk, the reins need to be shortened beforehand. On completion of the turn, they are lengthened again by the same amount.

To make a left turn the driver prepares the horses and shortens the strides. The left lead rein is then looped and placed under the driver's thumb to start the turn. A second loop is then made with the left lead rein, along with the left swing rein. To drive straight ahead again, the loops are released slowly, supported by the right hand. Before and during the turn, the inside (left) wheeler should be sent forward as required with strategically placed whip aids to ensure that it continues to pull the vehicle through the turn.

All turns with a six-in-hand depend on the reins being held absolutely securely in the left hand and the loops being made properly. Once the first pair has turned, the driver should drive the next pair as if to send them forward into the gap between the two horses in front. With a six-in-hand the problem of the wheelers making the vehicle cut the corner does not arise to the same extent as with a four-in-hand, since the swing pole 'opposes' the main pole, as it were. However, the driver still needs to keep a positive contact on the outside reins, though without preventing the horses from flexing correctly into the turn.

With a random, the reins are held and handled as for a six-in-hand. The lead reins must be handled with great sensitivity, but positively. It is rare to find an absolutely steady leader who will go forwards and straight without another horse next to him, and who will obey the driver's rein aids without hesitation.

FAULTS IN TEAM AND TANDEM DRIVING

All faults which occur in pair driving will become even more evident when driving teams, tandems, etc. Taking up the reins carelessly is a particularly bad fault when it occurs in team driving, because it means that when the horses move off they are not equally in work or correctly aligned. Also, if the driver does not take care to hold the reins securely in his left hand, and allows one or more of the reins to slip, the team will soon become unsettled and he will no longer be properly under control. If the brake is not used correctly, the bars may bang against the leaders' hind legs, which could cause them to kick or bolt. The driver of a team (or tandem) must be absolutely familiar with the handling of a team (or tandem) whip. Whips hanging down get in the way, inconvenience other road users, and can lead to accidents. If the driver is not skilled in using the whip on the leaders, he will upset the wheelers and make them impatient, while the leaders still hang back.

A common fault is too long lead reins. The leaders are then too much in draught, and the driver is not in proper control of the team.

Other faults are:

- the horses are not correctly aligned

- the leaders are not taken out of draught at the beginning of a turn, and the wheelers are not pointing towards the gap between the leaders

- the wheelers are poled up too tightly, so that there is pressure on their necks when the leaders are in draught

The most common driver faults are:

- moving off without releasing the brake, or failing to apply the brake before sitting down

- using the brake too much or too little, or not co-ordinating its use with the other aids

- moving off with the reins slack, failing to 'give' sufficiently with the reins or failing to keep a contact with the horses' mouths; whip in the socket instead of in the hand

- leaning forward when moving off, twisting the upper body, leaning back when stopping, sitting with the legs apart

- not adjusting the reins to match the gait, the degree of extension or collection, or workload

- consciously or unconsciously letting the reins slip; lengthening the reins by pulling them upwards through the left hand instead of slowly forwards in the direction of the horses' mouths

- 'giving' or lengthening the reins and losing the contact with the horses' mouths in the process

- pulling the inside rein in the turns (or even using the right hand to pull the left rein on left turns)

- coming back to a walk too late and failing to shorten the reins sufficiently prior to a tight right turn; failing to come back almost to a halt prior to a 'U' turn.

Appendix 1: Humane Treatment of Animals

Care and management

- Feeding and watering
- Stabling
- Grooming
- Shoeing
- Exercise
- Veterinary supervision
- Treatments and therapies

Specific considerations

- **Harness** (it should fit, not restrict the breathing or movement, and not cause pain)

- **Attachment to the vehicle** (the horse should be able to retain its balance, and its freedom of movement should not be impaired)

- **Handling and training methods** (knowledgeable handling; aids should not cause pain, constraint should not be used)

- **Work** (duration, speed and workload appropriate for the level of training and fitness)

- **Training system and environment** (training ground, driving on the roads and across country, transporting the horse; taking into account the horse's level of physical and mental preparation)

- **Fitness** (fitness training related to the chosen activity, e.g. competition, pleasure driving, long distance or show driving)

- **Doping** (no forbidden performance-enhancing substances, sedatives or pain-killers)

Sources/References

1. *Tierschutzgesetz* (The German animal protection regulations)
2. *Leistungs-Prüfungs-Ordnung* (*LPO*) (The German competition rule book)
3. *Leitlinien Tierschutz im Pferdesport* (Guidelines for humane treatment of horses in sport)
4. *Merkblatt DRV Nr.13* (DRV Information sheet No.13)
5. *Die ethischen Grundsätze des Pferdefreundes* (The horseman's duties to his horse)

Appendix 2: Accident Prevention checklist

1. IN THE STABLE

- No running in the stable corridor.
- Approach horses from the front.
- When approaching or before touching the horse always speak to it and await its reaction.
- Bring horses out of the stable for grooming.
- Lead horses with a suitable halter or headcollar, with a rope or lead rein attached. The rope must not be wound around the hand.
- Lead horses at a walk in the stable corridor. When turning a horse whilst leading it, the horse should always be turned away from the handler.
- Only tie the horse up to fixed objects. Never tie the horse up by the bit.
- Always tie the horse up with a quick-release knot or clip. *[In some countries, as an additional precaution, it is recommended that the horse be tied to a piece of (breakable) string attached to the wall or fixed object – Translator.]*
- Tie horses up facing in the same direction.
- Stand to one side when cleaning out the feet.
- Sweep up after cleaning out the feet (can cause you to slip).
- Poor or tactless grooming technique can startle the horse.
- Do not allow the harness to drag along the ground when carrying it.
- Wear sturdy shoes and suitable clothing.
- **No smoking**!

2. ON THE VEHICLE

- Get on or off the vehicle only at a halt. Exception: marathon/cross-country vehicles with a backstep.
- Face forwards when getting on, and backwards when getting off.

- Whilst the driver is getting up from his seat or sitting down, a groom or passenger should stand in front of the horses (though not directly in front of the pole) and should hold the horses if necessary by the reins, but not the bridles.

- Talk to the horses before touching them (because they are wearing blinkers!).

- When acting as groom or being carried as a passenger, sit quietly and:

- Avoid making any movements which could be wrongly interpreted as traffic signals.

- Do not fiddle with the whip.

- Do not touch the reins, brake or whip.

3. BEFORE AND AFTER THE DRIVE

- When leading a horse which is wearing harness, always watch and guide the horse through narrow entrances and passageways, and when leading it up to or away from the pole.

- Put the horses in and take them out facing away from the stable.

- The reins must not be tied to the vehicle or splinter bar.

INDEX

Page numbers in *italic* denote illustrations

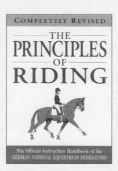

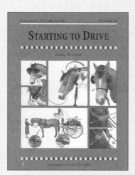
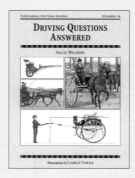
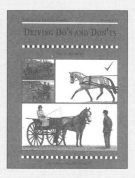